# THE
# HURON

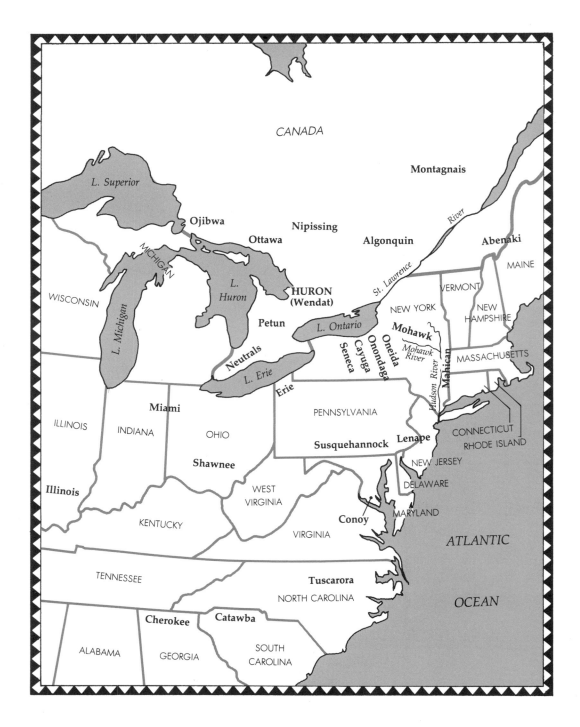

# THE
# HURON

*Nancy Bonvillain*
*State University of New York at Stony Brook*

Frank W. Porter III
*General Editor*

CHELSEA HOUSE PUBLISHERS
*New York   Philadelphia*

*On the cover*  Leather slippers with moosehair
embroidery made by Huron in Canada in 1911

**Chelsea House Publishers**
*Editor-in-Chief*  Nancy Toff
*Executive Editor*  Remmel T. Nunn
*Managing Editor*  Karyn Gullen Brown
*Copy Chief*  Juliann Barbato
*Picture Editor*  Adrian G. Allen
*Art Director*  Maria Epes
*Manufacturing Manager*  Gerald Levine

**Indians of North America**
*Senior Editor*  Marjorie P. K. Weiser

*Staff for* **THE HURON**
*Associate Editor*  Liz Sonneborn
*Deputy Copy Chief*  Nicole Bowen
*Editorial Assistant*  Claire Wilson
*Assistant Art Director*  Loraine Machlin
*Designer*  Donna Sinisgalli
*Designer Assistant*  James Baker
*Picture Researcher*  Margalit Fox
*Production Coordinator*  Joseph Romano

3  5  7  9  8  6  4  2

Library of Congress Cataloging-in-Publication Data

Bonvillain, Nancy.
The Huron / Nancy Bonvillain : Frank W. Porter III, general
editor.
    p.  cm.—(Indians of North America)
Bibliography: p.
Includes index.
Summary: Examines the history, culture, and changing
fortunes of the Huron Indians who made their home between
Lake Huron and Lake Ontario.
ISBN 1-55546-708-3
    0-7910-0382-5 (pbk.)
1. Huron Indians—Juvenile Literature. 2. Indians of North
America—Ontario—Juvenile literature. [1. Huron
Indians.  2. Indians of North America.] I. Porter, Frank W.,
1947 –      . II. Title. III. Series: Indians of North America
(Chelsea House Publishers)                        89-930
E99.H9B66  1989                                    CIP
971.3'00497—dc19                                   AC

# CONTENTS

Indians of North America:
Conflict and Survival  7
*by Frank W. Porter III*

1. Origins of the Wendat People  13
2. The Wendat World  21
3. Trading with the French  41
4. The Critical Years  51
5. From Huronia to Lorette  61
   *Picture Essay*
   Embroidery in Moosehair  65
6. The Huron of the West  79
7. The Huron and the Wyandot Today  97

   Bibliography  104
   The Huron at a Glance  105
   Glossary  106
   Index  108

# INDIANS OF NORTH AMERICA

The Abenaki

American Indian
   Literature

The Apache

The Arapaho

The Archaeology
   of North America

The Aztecs

The Cahuilla

The Catawbas

The Cherokee

The Cheyenne

The Chickasaw

The Chinook

The Chipewyan

The Choctaw

The Chumash

The Coast Salish Peoples

The Comanche

The Creeks

The Crow

The Eskimo

Federal Indian Policy

The Hidatsa

The Huron

The Iroquois

The Kiowa

The Kwakiutl

The Lenapes

The Lumbee

The Maya

The Menominee

The Modoc

The Montagnais-Naskapi

The Nanticoke

The Narragansett

The Navajos

The Nez Perce

The Ojibwa

The Osage

The Paiute

The Pima-Maricopa

The Potawatomi

The Powhatan Tribes

The Pueblo

The Quapaw

The Seminole

The Tarahumara

The Tunica-Biloxi

Urban Indians

The Wampanoag

Women in American
   Indian Society

The Yakima

The Yankton Sioux

The Yuma

CHELSEA HOUSE PUBLISHERS

# INDIANS OF NORTH AMERICA: CONFLICT AND SURVIVAL

## Frank W. Porter III

*The Indians survived our open intention of wiping them out, and since the tide turned they have even weathered our good intentions toward them, which can be much more deadly.*

John Steinbeck
*America and Americans*

When Europeans first reached the North American continent, they found hundreds of tribes occupying a vast and rich country. The newcomers quickly recognized the wealth of natural resources. They were not, however, so quick or willing to recognize the spiritual, cultural, and intellectual riches of the people they called Indians.

*The Indians of North America* examines the problems that develop when people with different cultures come together. For American Indians, the consequences of their interaction with non-Indian people have been both productive and tragic. The Europeans believed they had "discovered" a "New World," but their religious bigotry, cultural bias, and materialistic world view kept them from appreciating and understanding the people who lived in it. All too often they attempted to change the way of life of the indigenous people. The Spanish conquistadores wanted the Indians as a source of labor. The Christian missionaries, many of whom were English, viewed them as potential converts. French traders and trappers used the Indians as a means to obtain pelts. As Francis Parkman, the 19th-century historian, stated, "Spanish civilization crushed the Indian; English civilization scorned and neglected him; French civilization embraced and cherished him."

7

Nearly 500 years later, many people think of American Indians as curious vestiges of a distant past, waging a futile war to survive in a Space Age society. Even today, our understanding of the history and culture of American Indians is too often derived from unsympathetic, culturally biased, and inaccurate reports. The American Indian, described and portrayed in thousands of movies, television programs, books, articles, and government studies, has either been raised to the status of the "noble savage" or disparaged as the "wild Indian" who resisted the westward expansion of the American frontier.

Where in this popular view are the real Indians, the human beings and communities whose ancestors can be traced back to ice-age hunters? Where are the creative and indomitable people whose sophisticated technologies used the natural resources to ensure their survival, whose military skill might even have prevented European settlement of North America if not for devastating epidemics and disruption of the ecology? Where are the men and women who are today diligently struggling to assert their legal rights and express once again the value of their heritage?

The various Indian tribes of North America, like people everywhere, have a history that includes population expansion, adaptation to a range of regional environments, trade across wide networks, internal strife, and warfare. This was the reality. Europeans justified their conquests, however, by creating a mythical image of the New World and its native people. In this myth, the New World was a virgin land, waiting for the Europeans. The arrival of Christopher Columbus ended a timeless primitiveness for the original inhabitants.

Also part of this myth was the debate over the origins of the American Indians. Fantastic and diverse answers were proposed by the early explorers, missionairies, and settlers. Some thought that the Indians were descended from the Ten Lost Tribes of Israel, others that they were descended from inhabitants of the lost continent of Atlantis. One writer suggested that the Indians had reached North America in another Noah's ark.

A later myth, perpetrated by many historians, focused on the relentless persecution during the past five centuries until only a scattering of these "primitive" people remained to be herded onto reservations. This view fails to chronicle the overt and covert ways in which the Indians successfully coped with the intruders.

All of these myths presented one-sided interpretations that ignored the complexity of European and American events and policies. All left serious questions unanswered. What were the origins of the American Indians? Where did they come from? How and when did they get to the New World? What was their life—their culture—really like?

In the late 1800s, anthropologists and archaeologists in the Smithsonian Institution's newly created Bureau of American Ethnology in Washington,

D.C., began to study scientifically the history and culture of the Indians of North America. They were motivated by an honest belief that the Indians were on the verge of extinction and that along with them would vanish their languages, religious beliefs, technology, myths, and legends. These men and women went out to visit, study, and record data from as many Indian communities as possible before this information was forever lost.

By this time there was a new myth in the national consciousness. American Indians existed as figures in the American past. They had performed a historical mission. They had challenged white settlers who trekked across the continent. Once conquered, however, they were supposed to accept graciously the way of life of their conquerors.

The reality again was different. American Indians resisted both actively and passively. They refused to lose their unique identity, to be assimilated into white society. Many whites viewed the Indians not only as members of a conquered nation but also as "inferior" and "unequal." The rights of the Indians could be expanded, contracted, or modified as the conquerors saw fit. In every generation, white society asked itself what to do with the American Indians. Their answers have resulted in the twists and turns of federal Indian policy.

There were two general approaches. One way was to raise the Indians to a "higher level" by "civilizing" them. Zealous missionaries considered it their Christian duty to elevate the Indian through conversion and scanty education. The other approach was to ignore the Indians until they disappeared under pressure from the ever-expanding white society. The myth of the "vanishing Indian" gave stronger support to the latter option, helping to justify the taking of the Indians' land.

Prior to the end of the 18th century, there was no national policy on Indians simply because the American nation has not yet come into existence. American Indians similarly did not possess a political or social unity with which to confront the various Europeans. They were not homogeneous. Rather, they were loosely formed bands and tribes, speaking nearly 300 languages and thousands of dialects. The collective identity felt by Indians today is a result of their common experiences of defeat and/or mistreatment at the hands of whites.

During the colonial period, the British crown did not have a coordinated policy toward the Indians of North America. Specific tribes (most notably the Iroquois and the Cherokee) became military and political pawns used by both the crown and the individual colonies. The success of the American Revolution brought no immediate change. When the United States acquired new territory from France and Mexico in the early 19th century, the federal government wanted to open this land to settlement by homesteaders. But the Indian tribes that lived on this land had signed treaties with European governments assuring their title to the land. Now the United States assumed legal responsibility for honoring these treaties.

At first, President Thomas Jefferson believed that the Louisiana Purchase contained sufficient land for both the Indians and the white population. Within a generation, though, it became clear that the Indians would not be allowed to remain. In the 1830s the federal government began to coerce the eastern tribes to sign treaties agreeing to relinquish their ancestral land and move west of the Mississippi River. Whenever these negotiations failed, President Andrew Jackson used the military to remove the Indians. The southeastern tribes, promised food and transportation during their removal to the West, were instead forced to walk the "Trail of Tears." More than 4,000 men, woman, and children died during this forced march. The "removal policy" was successful in opening the land to homesteaders, but it created enormous hardships for the Indians.

By 1871 most of the tribes in the United States had signed treaties ceding most or all of their ancestral land in exchange for reservations and welfare. The treaty terms were intended to bind both parties for all time. But in the General Allotment Act of 1887, the federal government changed its policy again. Now the goal was to make tribal members into individual landowners and farmers, encouraging their absorption into white society. This policy was advantageous to whites who were eager to acquire Indian land, but it proved disastrous for the Indians. One hundred thirty-eight million acres of reservation land were subdivided into tracts of 160, 80, or as little as 40 acres, and allotted tribe members on an individual basis. Land owned in this way was said to have "trust status" and could not be sold. But the surplus land—all Indian land not allotted to individuals—was opened (for sale) to white settlers. Ultimately, more than 90 million acres of land were taken from the Indians by legal and illegal means.

The resulting loss of land was a catastrophe for the Indians. It was necessary to make it illegal for Indians to sell their land to non-Indians. The Indian Reorganization Act of 1934 officially ended the allotment period. Tribes that voted to accept the provisions of this act were reorganized, and an effort was made to purchase land within preexisting reservations to restore an adequate land base.

Ten years later, in 1944, federal Indian policy again shifted. Now the federal government wanted to get out of the "Indian business." In 1953 an act of Congress named specific tribes whose trust status was to be ended "at the earliest possible time." This new law enabled the United States to end unilaterally, whether the Indians wished it or not, the special status that protected the land in Indian tribal reservations. In the 1950s federal Indian policy was to transfer federal responsibility and jurisdiction to state governments, encourage the physical relocation of Indian peoples from reservations to urban areas, and hasten the termination, or extinction, of tribes.

Between 1954 and 1962 Congress passed specific laws authorizing the termination of more than 100 tribal groups. The stated purpose of the termination policy was to ensure the full and complete integration of Indians into American society. However, there is a less benign way to interpret this legislation. Even as termination was being discussed in Congress, 133 separate bills were introduced to permit the transfer of trust land ownership from Indians to non-Indians.

With the Johnson administration in the 1960s the federal government began to reject termination. In the 1970s yet another Indian policy emerged. Known as "self-determination," it favored keeping the protective role of the federal government while increasing tribal participation in, and control of, important areas of local government. In 1983 President Reagan, in a policy statement on Indian affairs, restated the unique "government is government" relationship of the United States with the Indians. However, federal programs since then have moved toward transferring Indian affairs to individual states, which have long desired to gain control of Indian land and resources.

As long as American Indians retain power, land, and resources that are coveted by the states and the federal government, there will continue to be a "clash of cultures," and the issues will be contested in the courts, Congress, the White House, and even in the international human rights community. To give all Americans a greater comprehension of the issues and conflicts involving American Indians today is a major goal of this series. These issues are not easily understood, nor can these conflicts be readily resolved. The study of North American Indian history and culture is a necessary and important step toward that comprehension. All Americans must learn the history of the relations between the Indians and the federal government, recognize the unique legal status of the Indians, and understand the heritage and cultures of the Indians of North America.

The excavation of a cluster of Iroquoian pottery fragments at the Pickering site near Toronto, Canada, in 1983. As the potsherds were removed, they were wrapped in aluminum foil to preserve them until they could be chemically tested to determine when they were made.

# ORIGINS
## OF THE
# WENDAT PEOPLE

Long ago, when there was only air and water, a woman named Aataentsic (ah-TANT-sik) lived in the sky as people now live on earth. One day she fell through a hole in the heavens and tumbled toward the waters below. To save Aataentsic from death, the animals in the water quickly gathered mud from the ocean bottom and piled it on the back of a large turtle. Aataentsic landed safely on this soft mound of mud, which became the Earth.

Soon after her fall, Aataentsic gave birth to twin boys, Iouskeha (you-SKE-ha) and Tawiscaron (da-WIS-ga-ron). They would help their mother create all things in the world. Aataentsic created human beings and is the caretaker of all people's souls. Iouskeha made corn and berries to eat and trees, rivers, and other good things for people to use. Tawiscaron, however, was ill tempered. He made monsters and tried to destroy the good things created by Iouskeha. Iouskeha had created rivers with two currents so that people could travel easily in both directions, but Tawiscaron made the water flow only

one way so that people would have a hard time paddling upstream. Eventually the brothers had a great battle, and Iouskeha was victorious. Now Aataentsic and Iouskeha live in a place far away where the souls of the dead visit on their journey to the afterworld.

This is one story that the Huron Indians tell about the creation of the world. The Huron are a confederacy of four tribes of Indians who traditionally lived in what is now southern Ontario, Canada. The name by which they are best known today was given to them by French traders in the 17th century. The Huron, however, called themselves the Wendat. In their language, Wendat means both "islanders" and "dwellers on a peninsula." This name reflects their belief that they were the people created by Aataentsic to inhabit the center of the great island Earth. It also refers to their traditional home on the land mass between what are today Georgian Bay and Lake Simcoe.

The Wendat were probably descendants of people who had lived in northeastern North America for thousands of

*The remains of an Iroquoian house from A.D. 1100 uncovered at the Pickering site. Each stake marks the location of a wooden post that served as a longhouse wall support.*

years. There is archaeological evidence that human communities existed in that region by about 10,000 B.C. Archaeologists have learned much about the origins of the Wendat by analyzing the remains of human life, such as tools, foods, and evidence of houses.

The earliest inhabitants of northeastern North America shared a way of life, referred to by archaeologists as the Eastern Woodland culture, that was based on food collecting. They gathered plant foods such as roots, berries, and wild rices, hunted for wild animals, and fished. Traveling in small groups, each composed of several families, they moved from place to place in pursuit of game and ripe vegetation, relying on seasonal changes to supply them with a variety of foods.

Over many years, these people developed new kinds of tools, new methods of obtaining food, and new forms of housing. Gradually their way of life, or culture, changed and became more secure and comfortable. To identify distinct culture differences, archaeologists look for changes in people's economies, village structures, and such things as housing, tools, and weapons.

One of the earliest cultures to emerge in northeastern North America is named for the Iroquoian language family, which consists of related languages spoken by many peoples living in the area. In general, archaeologists have identified four stages of this culture's development: pre-Iroquoian, before A.D. 1000; Early Iroquoian, from about 1000 to 1300; Middle Iroquoian, from about 1300 to 1400; and Late Iroquoian, from 1400 to 1500. At about that time Europeans first arrived in this part of North America and the historic period began.

Archaeologists have found evidence that the direct ancestors of the Huron were probably living in southern Ontario by about 500, in the pre-Iroquoian period. Until about 1000, these peoples continued to obtain all their food through gathering, hunting, and fishing. Their settlement patterns changed with the seasons. During the summer, when game and plant foods were plentiful, many people came together to live in relatively large camps. In the winter, when plants and animals became scarce, small groups of families left the camp, each going in a different direction in search of the little food available.

After 1000, the Indian groups in southern Ontario learned the techniques of farming that had been developed centuries before in what is now central Mexico. Corn was their first crop

## THE DEVELOPMENT OF IROQUOIAN CULTURES

| Period | Cultural development |
| --- | --- |
| Pre-Iroquoian, before A.D. 1000: | People lived in temporary camps, which they moved frequently in order to collect or hunt food according to its seasonal availability from natural sources. |
| Early Iroquoian, A.D. 1000–1300: | Groups of longhouses, constituting permanent villages surrounded by palisades, were first constructed. People had learned to cultivate corn but continued to collect other plant foods and to rely on fishing and hunting for meat. |
| Middle Iroquoian, A.D. 1300–1400: | Villages were planned and larger longhouses and thicker palisades were built. People learned to grow more crops, including sunflowers, and relied more on farming for food. Ritual may have become more important (some evidence suggests cannibalism, perhaps as part of victory celebrations), and communal burial was practiced. |
| Late Iroquoian, A.D. 1400–1500: | Larger longhouses and villages and thicker palisades were constructed. Beans and squash were cultivated as well as corn and sunflowers. Surplus crops were traded to nearby Indian groups. Villages were built closer together and in clusters. Neighboring villages formed alliances against common enemies. The Huron-Petun and the Neutral-Erie split into distinct divisions. |

and soon provided most of their food, although they continued to hunt and fish. The practice of agriculture marked the start of the Early Iroquoian period.

Obtaining food by farming had several advantages over food collection. It provided people with a reliable supply of a basic food, despite some variation in the size of their harvests from year to year due to changes in weather conditions. Their survival, unlike that of their ancestors, was not at the mercy of changes in the availability of wild plants and animals. Farming also made it both possible and necessary for people to live in more permanent villages. They no longer had to move from place to place every season to search for food. Rather, they had to stay within reach of their fields for most of the year in order to tend their crops. They could plant in the same fields for perhaps one

*A modern reconstruction of an Iroquoian longhouse. By the end of the prehistoric period, some of these Wendat dwellings were as long as 100 feet.*

*A model of an Iroquoian village. Longhouses were built parallel to each other in order to fit as many as possible within the area bounded by the village palisade.*

or two decades before depleting the soil's nutrients. Even then, as long as more land was available nearby to be cleared for new fields, people could remain in the same village.

Because they did not have to move frequently, the Early Iroquoians could build larger, sturdier homes and live together in larger communities. Village populations gradually increased as long as a community produced enough crops to feed additional people. Larger villages provided their inhabitants with greater security because there were more warriors in times of conflict. A greater concentration of population also allowed people to have more social contact and, therefore, more opportunities to form friendships, alliances, and marriages.

The basic structure of Wendat villages was first established during the Early Iroquoian period. Each village

consisted of a cluster of homes surrounded by fields. Beyond the fields was the hunting territory. The inhabitants lived in longhouses—large, rectangular dwellings built of cedar bark fastened to a wooden frame. Down the center of each ran a row of 10 to 12 hearths, each shared by the 2 families that lived on either side of it. In order to make it more difficult for intruders to attack their homes, the Early Iroquoians began to build their villages on the tops of hills instead of on the flatlands near rivers, as their ancestors had. They also built palisades or fences of wooden poles around the cluster of longhouses in every village for protection.

The Middle Iroquoian period, which began about 1300, was marked by greater reliance on farming and an increase in the size of the villages. The Middle Iroquoians began to grow an houses to be constructed as necessary on the fixed area within the palisade.

Warfare seems to have increased in this period. People built thicker palisades around their villages, which suggests that they had greater need for defense. Male prisoners were sometimes tortured and killed; fragments of cooked human bone that have been found at the site of some 14th-century Iroquoian villages suggest that dead enemies may also have been eaten in rituals of victory. Large ossuaries (pits containing human bones) from this period indicate that the Middle Iroquoians conducted communal burial ceremonies similar to those that were practiced in the historic period by the Huron and other Iroquoian people.

In the Late Iroquoian period, from about 1400, people learned to grow beans and squash as well as several hardier and more productive varieties of corn. Villages continued to become larger and to contain a greater number of longhouses, which also increased in size. Most houses found at 15th-century sites were at least 100 feet in length.

The Late Iroquoians used more and more poles to construct the palisades that surrounded their villages in order to provide more effective protection from enemies. The need for improved defenses also prompted them to build their villages closer to one another, sometimes only a mile or two apart. This proximity allowed inhabitants of one village to escape easily to a nearby one if their homes came under attack.

*Late Iroquoian artifacts: (a, b) pottery fragments; (c) stone pipe bowl; (d) deer antler harpoon; (e) stone scraper; (f) needle used to sew nets; (g) stone tortoise amulet; (h) stone and bone arrowheads; (i) pottery pipes; (j) dagger made from a human bone.*

important new plant, the sunflower, whose seeds they both ate and pressed to make an oil that they rubbed on their skin and hair to protect them in cold weather. Some villages became as large as 10 acres. At this time, the Iroquoians may have begun to plan for future increases in population by building longhouses parallel to one another, an arrangement that left space for more

Neighboring villages were also able to supply additional fighters without much delay.

As villages geographically close to one another started to form alliances to fight common enemies, Indian groups in different locations developed distinct identities. The similarities shared by Iroquoian people began to be elaborated on in different ways and in different regions. In the 15th century, two separate regional groups emerged: those who lived in the west, north of Lake Erie, and those who lived in the east, north of Lake Ontario. By 1500, tribes— societies bound together by common language, territory, and culture—had formed within these two divisions. In the western group were the Neutrals and the Erie. In the eastern group were the Petun and the four tribes of the Wendat Confederacy—the Attignawantan (the Bear People), the Attig-neenongnahac (the Cord People), the Tahontaenrat (the Deer People), and the Arendahronon (the Rock People).

The Wendat Confederacy probably began in the late 1400s or early 1500s when the Attignawantan and the Attigneenongnahac became allies. The two smaller Wendat tribes, the Tahontaenrat and the Arendahronon, joined the league considerably later, possibly not until about 1600. The political integration of these four neighboring Indian nations provided each of the Confederacy's members with security by guaranteeing that the tribes geographically closest to it were friendly. The Confederacy also discouraged enemies of any one tribe from attacking for fear that they would have to battle the combined forces of the entire league. With these bonds of mutual support in place, the stage was set for a common Wendat culture to emerge and flourish. ▲

*Scenes from Wendat life appeared on a map made in 1657 by Fran-*
*çois-Joseph Bressani, an Italian Jesuit priest who lived among the*
*Wendat during the winter of 1643. Pictured are men torturing a*
*war captive and a woman grinding corn outside a longhouse (shown*
*shorter than it actually would be).*

# THE
# WENDAT
# WORLD

In the 16th century the Wendat people developed a complex culture based on their beliefs about their relationship to their environment, their supernatural beings, and one another. We know about their life at that time because the first Europeans to travel through Wendat territory—French explorers and missionaries—wrote journals and letters describing their experiences among the tribes. In these documents, the French visitors recorded conversations they had with the Wendat through Indian interpreters. Because the Wendat did not have a written language, these are the only sources that exist today in which the Wendat of the time explained their own culture. These documents cannot be regarded as completely accurate, however. The writers viewed the Wendat with a European perspective and consequently did not always understand or approve of Indian habits and beliefs that did not conform to their own.

According to these sources, the Wendat numbered about 20,000 during the first decades of the 17th century. Their homeland measured approximately 35 miles from east to west and 20 miles from north to south. In this area were between 18 and 25 villages, the largest of which had a population of approximately 2,000. Most Wendat settlements were located near one of the many rivers and streams that flowed through their territory, making it easy to travel by canoe from one village to another. A series of well-used overland trails also connected the Wendat's settlements.

Like their Late Iroquoian ancestors, the Wendat obtained most of their food by farming. Their food crops included several varieties of beans and squash, but corn—the staple of the Wendat diet—was by far the most important crop. Although both men and women performed agricultural tasks, women did most of the labor in the fields.

Wendat men were responsible for preparing the fields for planting. To clear a plot of land, they first used stone axes to chop down small trees and to cut the branches from large ones. They then stripped the bark from around the large trunks near the base and burned the bare wood strip so the trunk would fall. The stumps left in the field eventually rotted, and the softened wood could be broken apart and easily removed. The wood from the rotten trunks was then used for various purposes.

The Wendat farmed the same fields every year for as long as they could. Men cleared new land nearby only when the soil in their fields was so depleted of nutrients that it could no longer produce a healthy crop. About every 10 to 20 years, all the land surrounding a village became infertile. The inhabitants would then have to move to another location. Wendat villages were also relocated when their inhabitants had used most of the trees in the vicinity for firewood or building material.

After men had cleared the fields, women took over the agricultural work. In the spring, they first removed any twigs or other debris from the land. Then, using wooden spades, they dug rows of small holes about 2 feet apart, into each of which they placed approximately 10 seeds. In advance of planting, women prepared the corn kernels that were to be used as seed by washing and soaking them in water for several days. All their food crops were grown in the same fields. Usually groups of related women—perhaps a woman and her daughters or several sisters—worked together on the same plot of

land or in nearby fields so they could keep each other company and help one another if necessary.

Throughout the summer, Wendat women carefully weeded the fields, and in the fall they harvested the crops. As they brought in the corn crop, they turned up the leaves around each cob and tied several together. Women hung these bundles from the poles that supported the roofs of their longhouses until the kernels became dry. They then shelled the cobs and stored the kernels in large casks inside their homes. The stored corn could be taken out of the casks and cooked whenever it was needed. Wendat women planted a surplus of corn each year to ensure that they would have a large enough crop to store a portion of it for use in a later year when the harvest might be small. The Wendat also traded extra corn with other tribes, especially the Algonquin to the north.

Because women's labor produced most of the Wendat's food, they were considered to own the harvest. Women therefore decided how the food they farmed would be divided among the members of their households. This was not difficult, however, because Wendat individuals rarely asked for more food than they needed.

Men did not plant food crops, but some grew tobacco in small plots in the fields. Tobacco was burned during many Wendat religious ceremonies and was sometimes smoked in elaborate pipes passed from person to person to seal a friendship or an alliance.

*A mortar (left) made from a hollowed tree stump and a wooden pestle, used by Wendat women to remove the kernels from corncobs.*

In addition to planting, tending, and harvesting the fields, Wendat women had several other important economic responsibilities. Working in groups, they gathered wild plants—particularly grapes, acorns, and onions—to add flavor and variety to their many corn dishes. Some fruits they gathered could be dried and kept for use throughout the year. The Wendat particularly liked strawberries and blackberries, which they often added to corn cakes and corn soups.

Several days every spring, all the women in each village went on an expedition to collect enough fallen tree limbs to provide firewood for their entire settlement for the next year. Sometimes they had to travel far to find dry wood, which they preferred because it produced little smoke when it was burned.

Running the household was another duty of Wendat women. Each day they usually prepared two meals—one in the morning and one in the early evening. Most meals consisted of one of the more than 20 different dishes made from boiled, roasted, or baked corn. Their most common dish was *sagamite* (sa-GA-mi-tey), a soup of boiled corn and water. Women sometimes flavored this mixture with berries, fish, or ashes from their hearth fire. From ground roasted corn, water, and sometimes berries, they made a batter that they baked to make bread or cakes. When they traveled, the Wendat often took baked corn with them to eat along their journey.

Women's chores also included making all household goods and clothing. From clay they molded pottery, which was hardened by baking in the sun and was used to cook and store food. From reeds and corn leaves, women wove mats that were used as seats and beds. From bark (usually birch bark) they sewed baskets and bowls. Women also sewed the softened skins of beaver, deer, and moose into robes, leggings, and moccasins. Sometimes they decorated clothing by painting it with various pigments made from plants or by embroidering designs on it with dyed porcupine quills.

*Engraving from Samuel de Champlain's* Voyages to New France *(published in 1632) showing the clothing of Wendat women. In the summer, they wore skirts of animal skin (left); in the winter, they added leggings and wrapped skins around their torsos. Champlain noted that the strings of shell beads they wore weighed as much as 12 pounds.*

Men made their most important contribution to the Wendat food supply by fishing. Throughout the year, different varieties of fish—including trout, sturgeon, and whitefish—were plentiful in the lakes, rivers, and streams that flowed through Wendat territory. Often, especially in the autumn, groups of men went on fishing expeditions. On these trips, they stretched nets across streams or narrow parts of lakes each evening and hauled in their catch the next morning. When lakes froze in the winter, men fished by making holes in the ice and dropping into the water nets or hooks attached to fishing lines made of hemp. The Wendat either ate fish fresh or allowed it to dry to preserve it for use at a later time.

Wendat men also hunted beavers, deer, and bears, especially in the fall. Although the Indians liked animal meat, it was a small part of the tribes' diet. Hunting was more important to the Wendat as a means of obtaining animal skins, which they needed as material for clothing and as goods to trade with other tribes.

Men used traps or bows and arrows to hunt large game as well as small animals such as rabbits, muskrats, and turtles. To capture a large number of animals at one time, they staged drives in which many people, often all the able-bodied men and women in a village, took part. The participants in an animal drive first formed two lines that came together at one end to create a V-shape. In this formation, they marched toward a group of animals and made loud noises to frighten them. When the animals were trapped in the tip of the V, they could easily be killed with arrows. The Wendat also built triangular wooden enclosures to capture animals, especially deer, using this principle.

Wendat men made all the tools they used to fish and hunt. They manufactured traps, bows, and arrow shafts from various kinds of wood, and arrowheads and knife and hatchet blades from stone and animal bone. They wove fishing nets from wild hemp that women had collected and twisted into strong twine.

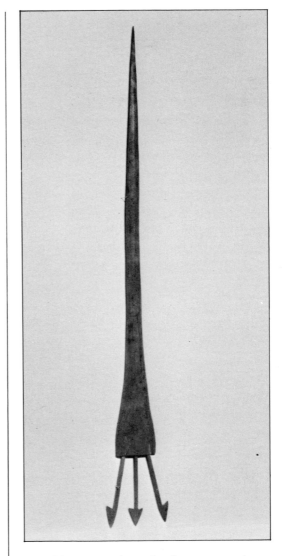

*Wendat men used wooden harpoons such as this to spear fish in frozen lakes and rivers.*

Men also made the clay tobacco pipes that they used in the rituals held before they went on hunting or fishing expeditions. At these ceremonies, Wendat men prayed and smoked tobacco as an offering to the spirits of the animals and fish they hoped to catch. They believed that animals were willing to be caught in order to help people survive, and their prayers thanked the animal spirits for this sacrifice on their behalf. The Wendat were also extremely careful not to burn animal bones when they cooked fish or meat. They feared that the souls of the animals they had killed would be angered by this maltreatment of their corpses and would report it to living animals, who would then not allow hunters to capture them.

Perhaps the most important economic activity of Wendat men was trading with neighboring tribes. The Wendat traded corn to Neutral and Pe-

*Wendat hunters staging a deer drive, as illustrated in Champlain's* Voyages to New France. *The enclosure in the drawing should be longer according to Champlain's own description; the walls actually stretched approximately half a mile.*

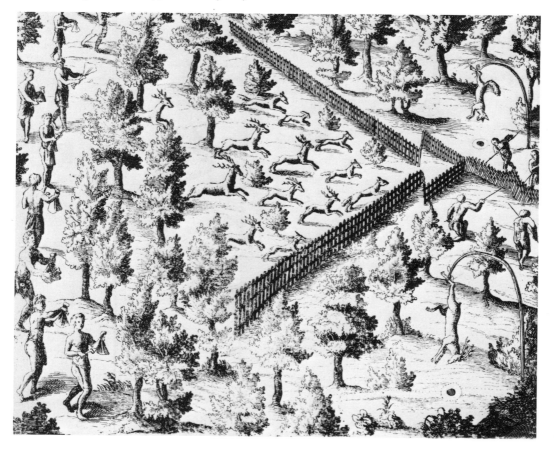

tun Indians to the southwest for squirrel skins and tobacco, which grew better in these tribes' warmer climate. From tribes to the north, such as the Nipissing and Algonquin, the Wendat obtained beaver and moose skins and fish in exchange for cornmeal. Groups of men traveled together in trading expeditions, but whenever they arrived in a foreign village each man dealt individually with the trading partners he had established there. Such visits were occasions for elaborate feasts, ceremonial speeches of welcome, and the exchange of gifts. When foreign traders came to Wendat villages, they were greeted with similar hospitality.

The Wendat people interacted with each other on the basis of social principles of kinship and friendship. Every Wendat belonged to one of eight clans, each of which was named for an animal such as the bear, wolf, or turtle. People in the same clan believed that they were descended from the same ancestor and had stories about this common ancestor and the clan's origin in the distant past. Wendat clans were matrilineal; clan members traced their descent through their mothers back to the original clan ancestor. Children were always members of their mother's clan.

All land was owned by clans, not by individuals. Each clan controlled a portion of the Wendat's farmland. Each adult had a right to clear and farm as much land from the clan's territory as he or she needed, but no one could intrude on the territory of other clans.

People had a claim to a field for as long as they farmed it. If they abandoned the land, however, any other member of their clan had the right to plant it.

Clans also owned the longhouses in which their members lived. Usually the residents of each longhouse were a group of sisters, their husbands and children, and their adult daughters' families. The Wendat had a matrilocal residence system in which married couples lived in the household of the wife's mother. Most men, however, remained close to their own clan and relatives because they usually married someone from the same or a nearby village.

Clan membership determined the selection of marriage partners. Because a man and woman belonging to the same clan were considered close relatives, they could not marry each other. Instead, each had to marry someone from another clan. In addition, the Wendat could not marry any other known relative of either their mother or father, even if the relative belonged to a different clan.

When a young woman and man decided they wanted to marry, the man first brought gifts to the woman's family as a show of his respect. He also gave her a special present, such as a beaverskin robe or a bead necklace. If the woman and her family accepted these tokens, her family planned a feast and invited the couple's relatives and friends. There the woman's father announced her desire to marry. When all those in attendance expressed their ap-

## THE ORIGIN OF THE SNAKE CLAN

*The members of each of the traditional Wendat clans had a story of how their clan came to be, which they passed down orally from generation to generation. In 1911, linguist Marius Barbeau recorded the origin story of the Snake clan as told to him by Smith Nichols, a man of Wendat descent.*

"An old woman was living with her granddaughter and taking care of her. One day, [the woman] went out to the woods, erected a hut, and secluded her grandchild in it. The girl was to fast until she would find and secure [special] powers. After she had been without food for ten days, she found the Snake, who spoke to her. 'Now you must eat: otherwise I will bring you along with me.' The old guardian came back to see the girl, who at once said, 'Grandmother, now I should eat: otherwise the Snake is going to bring me along with him.' The grandmother did not believe it and went away as usual, only to return in the evening of the next day. As soon as she had seen her granddaughter, she noticed that her legs were becoming fastened together while she was making a lake. Running back home, the woman got some food, and in haste she took it over to her secluded grandchild. The girl said, 'No! the time is now past.' She had become a snake up to the waist. 'Tomorrow at noon,' she added, 'you must be here, all of you who belong to my family, for you will all be present when the Snake gives you the charm on which shall depend your welfare.'

"The next day, they all proceeded to the woods, where the girl was secluded. As they arrived there, they saw that she had finished making a lake, and they stood along its shore. Now the water rose, and the Snake and the Indian maiden came out of the lake, twisted together. The Snake gave to the people its own shining scales as charms to be used for their welfare, and spoke to them, advising that they must . . . promise [to] have a feast every year. It also showed them the songs intended for [the] dance [to be performed at the feast], which they pledged themselves to hold yearly for their own security."

Source: Marius Barbeau,
"Huron-Wyandot Traditional Narratives."
Ottawa: National Museum of Canada,
Bulletin 165, 1960.

*A watercolor of a Wendat couple, painted by an unknown artist in the 18th century.*

proval, the couple was considered to be husband and wife.

Wendat spouses were expected to respect and cooperate with one another and enjoy each other's company. But if for any reason a wife or a husband wanted to end a marriage, the couple was free to separate. Divorce was fairly common among young people, but after spouses had children they were more likely to stay together.

Children were treated with much affection and indulgence by adults. Because the Wendat strongly believed in personal freedom, parents never forced children to behave in a particular man-

ner by threatening them physically or verbally. Children learned the rules of acceptable behavior instead by observing other people's actions and following their example. As children grew up, they also gradually became familiar with the skills that they would need as adults by watching their parents work. Girls helped their mothers weed the fields and cook meals, and boys accompanied their fathers on fishing and hunting expeditions.

Although women and men performed different roles in Wendat society, they were considered equals. Women took part with men in religious ceremonies and were looked to for their spiritual and curing abilities. The elder women who were heads of large families in each clan were particularly respected. Among these matrons' responsibilities was organizing the work of their households and dividing clan lands. People often sought their opinions and advice because of their experience as well as their knowledge, generosity, and good nature. The matrons also selected the chiefs who represented each clan at village, tribal, and Confederacy councils and could recall and demote a chief with whom the people were dissatisfied.

The council in each village was composed of a group of male elders and chiefs from every clan. This group met frequently to discuss everyday matters such as feasts, public games, and funerals and to solve local problems and disputes. Each chief was the headman of a clan. If a civil chief was demoted

*A Wendat village council, drawn by François-Joseph Bressani in 1657. At the beginning of each meeting, council members smoked pipes filled with tobacco because they believed the smoke would give them insight into the problems they were to discuss.*

or died, his position was often passed on to one of his sister's sons, who were also members of his clan. His own sons belonged to their mother's clan and therefore could not inherit the chieftainship. The clan matrons selected as chief an older man who was highly respected. They would choose a person who was generous, intelligent, and articulate and best exemplified the ideals of the people.

Each Wendat village also had a war chief, who organized the defense of the village and planned attacks against its enemies. War chiefs were usually younger than civil chiefs and earned their positions by bravery and success in warfare.

Several times a year, all the civil chiefs in each Wendat tribe would travel to its largest village to attend a tribal council. There they would discuss issues of concern to the entire tribe, such as community ceremonies, and settle disputes among its people or villages. Because chiefs from several villages represented each clan at tribal councils, clans designated their most respected leader as their speaker. Before an issue was addressed at the tribal council, all the chiefs of a clan discussed it informally among themselves and came to some agreement. The clan's speaker then presented this view at the general meeting. If all the speakers expressed the same position, the matter was settled. More often, however, the speakers did not agree. Then the chiefs of each clan discussed the issue again, taking into account all the various points that had been argued by the speakers. The clan chiefs then revised their positions, which their speakers presented during the next session of the tribal council. Discussions continued in this manner until all tribal council representatives reached a consensus.

This complex political process reflected some of the most important values of Wendat society. The Wendat believed that no one had the right to force other people to do anything or tell them how to behave. Although they valued others' advice, they believed that all people should be free to form opinions for themselves. This principle ruled not only their political order but also all Wendat social relationships.

*Wendat men dressed for warfare. The figure on the left carries a cedar-bark shield. The warrior on the right wears armor made from slats of wood laced together with cord to protect himself from the arrows of enemy Indians.*

Every year in the spring, the members of the four tribal councils of the Wendat Confederacy gathered for several weeks to discuss matters of importance to all of them, especially trade with foreigners, warfare against enemies, and disputes among member tribes. The same process used to reach a consensus at the tribal councils was used at these sessions. Confederacy meetings also served an important social function, as chiefs used this time to renew friendships with each other and spectators met members of other tribes. Because the Wendat considered friendship necessary for all political and trade alliances, this socializing helped to strengthen the Confederacy.

The Wendat frequently fought with other Indian groups. Most of their skirmishes with their neighbors were motivated by blood feuds. Whenever a Wendat was murdered by a person in another tribe, the relatives of the victim felt obligated to avenge the slaying by attacking the killer or his or her relatives. The families of the victims of these attacks were then bound to retaliate. Blood feuds often continued for long periods of time, as each side sought to inflict new casualties to avenge the other's previous assault.

Wendat military expeditions were led by the various war chiefs of each tribe, who sometimes traveled from village to village to gain the support of as many people as possible. Warriors chose for themselves whether to join a particular war party and usually volunteered only when they respected the leader and his plans. Young men gained great prestige in battle by acting with bravery and daring and by bringing prisoners back to their villages. Women and children who were taken captive were usually adopted by families who had lost relatives in warfare, but male prisoners were more often tortured to death in public displays of victory.

To gain success in battle, warriors sometimes prayed or made offerings of tobacco to the sky. The Wendat believed that the sky, as well as other natural elements, including the sun, moon, and thunder, possessed *oki*, a special supernatural power over people's lives. The sky's oki was the most powerful because it controlled the seasons and the weather.

Certain Wendat, especially famous chiefs, warriors, or healers, were thought to have oki. These people could obtain their power in several different ways. Some fasted for many days and then saw supernatural visions, from which they learned secret songs and prayers. Others gained oki through unusual dreams. Still others found special charms, such as feathers, owl's claws, or peculiarly shaped stones, that were filled with power. To the Wendat, success and supernatural power were always linked: Power gave success, and success was a sign of power.

The Wendat believed that all living beings, natural forces, and some inanimate objects had souls. They held ritual feasts throughout the year to gain the aid of these spirits or to thank them for past favors. For instance, people often held curing feasts when they contracted a serious illness and staged a thanksgiving feast if they recovered. Wendat who believed that they were soon going to die sometimes gave a farewell feast for relatives and friends. Although the hosts of most Wendat feasts ate little or nothing at all, the dying person at a farewell feast dined on the best food served.

The Wendat's grandest feasts were singing feasts held to honor new chiefs, to begin a war expedition, or to celebrate a military victory. Hundreds of people, including many chiefs from all the clans, were invited to these events, which often lasted for several days. Guests sang and danced and were served delicacies of soup and stews made with bear or dog meat. The person who arranged a feast, who was usually an important chief, always made sure that food was plentiful and that all guests were well fed.

Dances were also popular social and religious occasions with the Wendat. They were held throughout the year for one of four purposes: to ask spirits for help, to welcome visitors, to celebrate a victory, or to prevent or cure a serious illness. Adult men and women danced at these events, and the elderly and children were enthusiastic spectators. At both dances and feasts, respected elders recited the Wendat's ancient stories about the creation of the world and the adventures of spirits to entertain and educate their grandchildren.

Some Wendat men and women were believed to have special kinds of supernatural talents, such as an ability to foretell the future or to find lost objects. Curers were the most important of these special people. Prevention of disease and curing the ill were of great concern to the Wendat and provided the basis of many of their religious beliefs and practices.

Some Wendat curers specialized in diagnosing ailments and recommending treatments that another healer would then perform. The Wendat recognized that ailments could be caused by several different factors, so these specialists used a variety of methods to reach the correct diagnoses for their patients' illnesses. These included observing the patient's physical and mental condition; analyzing the dreams of the ill person; and gazing into water or fire or going into a trance, during which the

*A rattle made from a deer horn, leather, and feathers. Rattles such as this were used during Wendat rituals and dances.*

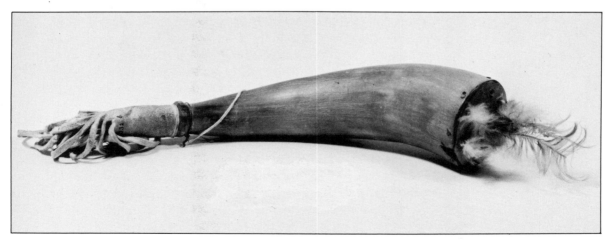

*A Wendat dance to cure the sick.*

curer might see a sign or symbol of the ailment's cause.

When Wendat curers diagnosed an illness as due to natural causes, they usually prescribed a remedy made from one of the various herbs and roots that the Wendat knew were of medicinal value. For instance, they placed wild sarsaparilla on sores or burns to make them heal quickly. They also made a tea from ground turnips for the patients with head colds to drink.

When patients were nasty, stingy, or held grudges against others, curers blamed witchcraft for their condition. Some people were said to be evil and able to cast spells by magically inserting harmful charms into the bodies of their victims. To remove spells, healers located the dangerous object, which was usually a piece of bone, a human nail, a pebble, or a feather, by placing their hands or mouth on the patients and then magically drew or sucked the charms out of their bodies.

The Wendat also believed that denying a hidden desire could make a person ill. Like modern psychologists, they thought that information about such desires was contained in dreams. Wendat curers used dream analysis to prevent disease and to diagnose an illness and prescribe an effective cure.

Wendat people generally could understand many of their dreams and the desires expressed in them. But to comprehend the hidden meaning of more obscure dreams, they sometimes consulted a curer who specialized in dream interpretation. As soon as their dreams had been explained, they then tried to satisfy their desire in order to prevent the illness or misfortune that might result if the wish were left unfulfilled. Often dreamers elicited the help of relatives and friends. If, for instance, a Wendat desired an object, such as a piece of clothing or a tool, the dreamer might ask a friend to donate it. If a dreamer wished for a feast or dance, his or her family or even an entire village might work together to stage the event.

The Wendat believed that nightmares could reveal dangerous "desires" that could be satisfied by acting out the dream symbolically. For instance, if a warrior dreamed he was captured and tortured by his enemies, his friends might tie him up and burn his feet or hands just long enough to inflict pain without doing lasting harm. By dramatizing a feared event, the Wendat thought they could prevent it from actually happening.

Dream analysis played a key role in a Wendat ceremony called the Ononharoia (o-non-ha-RO-ya), which means "turning the brain upside down." This ritual was held in each village at least once every winter, but it was sometimes performed at another time of the year if someone in the village dreamed about the ceremony. During the Ononharoia, groups of villagers ran from house to house, making as much noise as they could. At each house, the participants would ask the inhabitants to guess what they had dreamed the night before and to give them the object that their dreams revealed they desired. The dreamers gave hints of what they wanted in the form of riddles and collected objects until someone offered the desired item. They then returned all the other articles to their original owners. This lively ceremony was performed to keep a village population healthy by fulfilling its inhabitants' wishes en masse, but it also functioned as a means of drawing the community together for a festival of gift giving.

Curing rituals were also performed by organizations composed of members from many different clans and villages who specialized in the treatment of a particular ailment. Some people inherited membership in these curing societies, but others joined one after they had been successfully treated by its members. In one curing society ritual, members dressed in animal skins and crawled on the floor around the ailing person. In another, the curers wore wooden or straw masks and shook rattles to force the spirits that were causing the disease to leave the bodies of their patients.

The most elaborate curing-society ritual was the Awataerohi. During this ceremony, some curers warmed their hands by rubbing or holding red-hot coals and then placed their heated hands on the part of the patient's body that was diseased. Meanwhile other society members put hot stones in their mouths and made wild-animal noises in the ill person's ear. Still others blew ashes or bits of hot charcoal at the patient. Throughout this ritual, the specialists made loud noises to frighten away the disease-causing spirits. Sometimes members of curing societies also went into mild trances brought on by their dancing, singing, and general excitement.

The Wendat believed that the Awataerohi was particularly effective in curing many ailments, and it was therefore frequently prescribed by their curers. But the effectiveness of all their curing-society rituals depended largely on the people's belief in their power. These

## HURON KINSHIP TERMINOLOGY

Kinship is the network of relationships among people who are biologically and socially related. Every society has a system of terms that denote kinship (such as mother, sister, uncle, and so on). Kinship terms reflect both the relationships among a group's members and the way the society organized the interactions of its members.

Kinship terms indicate aspects of relationships that are important in the society. They almost always indicate the generation of a relative—mother and uncle are a generation older than we are; sister and cousin are of our own generation; son and niece are a generation younger. Some terms indicate gender: Grandfather, uncle, brother, and son are all males. Cousin, however, may be either male or female. In mainstream American society these distinctions are important and dictate the nature of personal interactions among these people. In other societies other distinctions and interactions may be of equal or greater importance, and some of the distinctions we make may be of little or no importance.

The Huron's kinship system reflected the organization of their society into clans made up of many families. Clan membership was matrilineal, traced through the mother's side of the family, and Huron kinship expressed this. For instance, the two Huron words *anan* and *ondouen* both meant "mother" and "mother's sister." This was because a person's mother and maternal aunt were members of the same clan in the same generation and could fill either role for each other's children. For the same reason, the words for "father" (*aystan* and *aihtaha*) were also used for "father's brother" because both the father and the paternal uncle belonged to the same clan and were of the same generation. A woman referred to her sister's children as her sons or daughters but called the children of her husband's brother her nieces or

complex ceremonies required a great deal of preparation, energy, and occasionally risk on the part of many people in a community. This attention and care gave patients a psychological boost that often contributed to their cures.

When treatments failed, Wendat patients were expected to face death bravely. They sometimes helped plan their own funerals and gave farewell feasts for their relatives. But however stoically dying people behaved, their

nephews because they belonged to a clan different than her own. She would never be expected to be a mother to the children of her husband's relatives because they were not members of the same clan.

The chart indicates the rules of kinship and descent in the Huron kinship system.

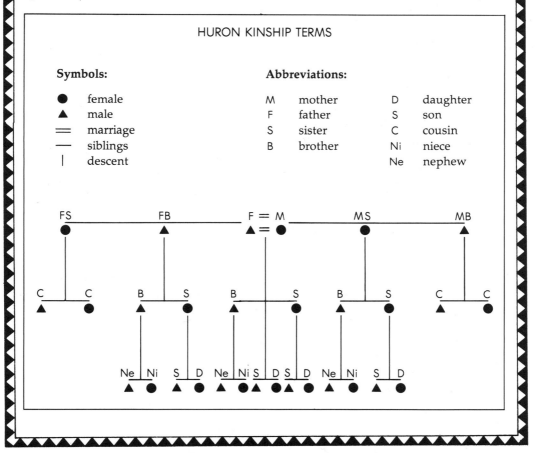

relatives and other villagers expressed sadness and mourned deeply at their passing.

A corpse was usually buried three days after death. Friends of the deceased or relatives from other clans were responsible for making the burial arrangements because the person's close relatives were often too overcome by grief to do so. The body was either buried in the ground with stakes surrounding it to mark the spot or placed

*A drawing of a Wendat burial from Champlain's memoirs. The corpse is in the bark coffin that rests on the raised platform. The ornamentation of the posts that support the platform and the chimneys on the top of the longhouse in the distance are products of the European artist's imagination.*

in a bark coffin on a raised platform supported by 4 8-to-10-foot-tall posts. People attending the funeral brought gifts of clothing, tools, and food, some of which were buried or entombed with the corpse to comfort the deceased's soul. The remainder was distributed among the dead person's relatives and the other guests. The spouse of the deceased continued to mourn for 10 days after the funeral by lying facedown on the ground and refusing to speak or to eat anything but cold food.

Every 10 years, the Feast of the Dead was performed in the largest village of each Wendat tribe. During this ritual, the most solemn and sacred of all Wendat ceremonies, the bones of people who had died in the preceding decade were unearthed and reburied in a common ossuary. Women were responsible for exhuming their relatives' bones, which they stripped of any remaining flesh and wrapped in beaver skins. They then carried the bundles in solemn processions to the village hosting the feast. There a large pit had been dug in preparation and lined with animal skins and presents, such as clothing, ornaments, and household goods, for the souls of the dead. The Wendat placed the bundles of bones into this mass grave, covered them with dirt, and drove wooden stakes into the ground surrounding the pit. The participants then held a sacred feast, after which they returned to their own villages.

The Wendat performed the Feast of the Dead in order to free the souls of the deceased. They believed that only after people's bones were placed in an ossuary could their souls leave the village where they were buried and journey to the afterworld. The activities and desires of souls were much like those of living people. The gifts given to souls during the Feast of the Dead, therefore, were intended to help them farm, fish, hunt, and hold feasts and ceremonies in the land of the dead.

The Feast of the Dead also benefited the living, however, by providing an emotional outlet for their grief. The ceremony bound the Wendat people together by giving them a common resting place in death and a common focus of interaction and support in life.

The unity of the Wendat was enforced by all aspects of their culture. As early explorers' journals indicate, the first Europeans to encounter them were fascinated by the complexity of the religious, political, social, and economic systems that the Wendat had constructed to order their world. But the more foreigners came among the Wendat, the more they changed the very customs that had so intrigued them initially. After less than 50 years of European contact, the Wendat homeland would be desolate and a single, unified culture would no longer exist. ▲

*The landing of Jacques Cartier in New France for his final North American expedition in 1542, shown on a 1547 map drawn by French cartographer Nicholas Vallard.*

# TRADING
## WITH
# THE FRENCH

In 1534 the French explorer Jacques Cartier traveled westward from the mouth of the St. Lawrence River. He was in search of a water route to Asia, but instead he discovered a region rich in natural resources bordering on the river, especially in what is now southeastern Canada.

Of particular interest to Cartier was the abundant beaver population. Beaver coats and hats were greatly desired by Europeans of the period; therefore, beaver pelts were worth considerable sums in European markets. Along the St. Lawrence, Cartier also encountered Indian hunters from several tribes who were skilled in trapping beavers and cleaning pelts. The explorer found that they were eager to trade the pelts to him in exchange for inexpensive goods he had brought with him from Europe. These transactions marked the beginning of the French fur trade in North America. This trade would continue for nearly three centuries, dramatically changing the lives of all the Indians in the region.

Throughout the late 16th and early 17th centuries, Cartier's experiences in-spired many French traders to rush to the St. Lawrence River area. Soon even the tribes that did not deal directly with the French learned of European manufactured goods from those who did. Probably by 1603, the Wendat were introduced to these items by their traditional northern trading partners who had become allies of the French, including the Algonquin and the Nipissing. These were Algonkian tribes; they had similar cultures and spoke related languages, which are all now classified as part of the Algonquian language family. The Algonkians traded the Wendat a variety of French products, including clothing, beads, and some prepared foods, such as wheat biscuits and dried fruit. But the French goods prized most by the Wendat were cooking pots, knives, tools, and other items made of iron, copper, or brass. Wendat women had made their cooking vessels and other containers out of baked clay. Wendat men had traditionally made arrow points and hatchet blades from stone. Iron pots were more durable and held heat better than pots made of clay. Tools made from metals were more effective than those of stone. Wendat men learned to fashion arrowheads from pieces of metal. The Wendat soon became eager to deal directly with French traders in order to obtain more of these treasured iron goods.

Mutual friendship with Algonkian traders provided the basis for the first meeting between the Wendat and the French explorer Samuel de Champlain in 1609. Champlain, who had learned from the Algonkians of the Wendat's interest in obtaining French products, asked to be introduced to some Wendat traders. The Wendat called Champlain and his men *agnonha* (agh-NON-ha), meaning "the iron people." The French were not so polite in the name they gave the Wendat. They referred to the Indians as the *Huron* and their territory as *Huronia*. Derived from the French word *hure*, literally "boar," Huron meant "savage" in colloquial French of the period.

The first Huron to meet Champlain were from the Arendahronon tribe, the easternmost member of the Huron Confederacy and the one geographically closest to the trading post the Frenchman had established at Quebec. According to Huron rules of trade, the Arendahronon had exclusive rights among the Huron to deal with the French because they had made the first contact with Champlain. By 1611, however, French goods were so important to all Huron that during a Confederacy council the Arendahronon offered to allow the other three tribes to negotiate with the Europeans.

In addition to giving the Huron a means of obtaining metal goods, their dealings with Champlain provided them with a military ally. In the early 1600s, the greatest enemies of the Huron and neighboring Algonkian peoples were the five nations of the Iroquois Confederacy (the Mohawk, Oneida, Onondaga, Cayuga, and Seneca), which were located south of the St. Lawrence River in what is now New York State. Hoping to gain control of the river and its tributaries and thus the trade route to and from Quebec, the Iroquois continually attacked the tribes to the north. In these raids the Iroquois also stole iron goods, which were otherwise difficult for them to obtain from French-allied Indians. Champlain preferred to deal with the Huron and the Algonkians because the pelts of beavers trapped in the cooler climate of these tribes' homelands were thicker. To keep his allies happy, he agreed not to negotiate with the Iroquois and occasionally to join his trading partners in battling these enemies.

The Huron first enlisted Champlain's military support in a 1609 campaign against the Mohawk, the people of the easternmost of the Iroquois nations. Huron traders sought revenge for the Mohawk's frequent attacks on their trading expeditions. In Champlain's memoirs of his voyages to North America, he described how his war party, which included some Hurons and Algonkians as well as his French troops, set out for Mohawk territory. This group of about 60 people separated into

*An engraving of Champlain and his Huron and Algonkian allies' 1609 attack on the Mohawk. Although this illustration is often attributed to Champlain, it was probably made long after the battle by a French artist: The canoes, which resemble French riverboats, and the palm trees, which are characteristic of Central and South America, indicate that it is not the work of an eyewitness.*

3 sections. One was made up of hunters, who supplied food along the journey; another of scouts, who looked out for enemy camps; and the last and largest, of the warriors who were to fight the battle. These groups traveled separately by day until they were two or three days' distance from the enemy. Then the three came together and continued their journey at night. During the day they rested and did not set fires or hunt for fear that the Mohawk would discover their approach. On these last days before the battle, they ate baked corn that had been prepared in advance, before they left home.

Several Indians in the war party who were expert fortune-tellers noticed omens or interpreted dreams that suggested that their mission would be successful. On the day before the battle, they asked Champlain about his dreams. He reported that during his sleep the previous night he had seen an Iroquois warrior drowning in a lake. This dream encouraged the Huron and other Indians in the party, who believed that it was a good sign.

The Huron were in fact successful in the next day's battle. Champlain wrote that the Iroquois were extremely frightened after he shot and killed two of their leaders. The Iroquois had never before seen guns and were so stunned by the sudden deaths of their warriors and by the loud noise the weapons made when fired that they were easily overcome. This victory and another successful campaign against the Mohawk the following year helped to solidify the Huron's alliance with the French.

In 1610, Champlain arranged an "exchange program" between the Huron and the French as a symbol of their allegiance. A Huron man known as Savignon to the French agreed to accompany Champlain on a trip to France to meet King Louis XIII and to learn about European life. In return, the Huron took in Étienne Brulé, a young Frenchman who had been living for two years at Champlain's post at Quebec. During Brulé's stay among the Huron he learned their language, and he later became an interpreter.

Savignon's experience in France was not so fruitful. Although he enjoyed a friendly and respectful reception at the royal court, he was repelled by many aspects of life among Europeans. He was particularly shocked by the harsh physical punishment of French children, the beating of prisoners, public arguments, and people begging for food in the streets, all of which were unknown among the Huron. Savignon soon returned to North America. Although he reported to the Huron that he had been well treated by his French hosts, he never expressed a desire to return to Europe.

In 1615, Champlain made an extended journey to Huronia and visited most of its large villages. The purpose of his trip was to strengthen his trading alliances with the Indians there by establishing the personal relationships the Huron valued as an assurance of their ally's support. Champlain was accompanied on this journey by Joseph LeCaron, a Catholic priest of the Recollet order, who became the first of many missionaries to visit and preach to the Huron. The Huron welcomed LeCaron as they had Étienne Brulé and all other temporary European visitors. Several Huron families even asked to adopt the priest. LeCaron instead requested that the Huron build him a cabin at the edge of their villages. The Indians complied and LeCaron remained among them for several months. During this time the priest learned to speak a little of the Huron language and began to compile a Huron dictionary.

Despite the Huron's graciousness toward the priest, they had little interest in the Christian teachings of LeCaron and the other priests who soon followed him to Huronia. A French Recollet missionary, Gabriel Theodat de Sagard, described in his journal the Huron's hospitality during his visit to Huronia in 1622–23:

(continued on page 48)

# CHAMPLAIN'S ACCOUNT OF THE BATTLE OF 1615

*On October 10, 1615, the Huron, the Algonkians, and Samuel de Champlain and his men joined forces to attack an Iroquois village near the present-day city of Syracuse, New York. This was Champlain's last joint campaign with the Huron. A former officer in the French army, Champlain became frustrated with the Indians when they would not fight according to European rules of combat. Throughout the battle, he repeatedly reprimanded them, speaking in French because he knew no Indian languages. When his commands went unheeded, he concluded that the Huron and the Algonkians were undisciplined warriors.*

*Just as Champlain had never bothered to learn the Indians' languages, he also had made no effort to understand the nature of Indian warfare. Unlike European soldiers, Huron and Algonkian warriors did not fight in order to capture their enemies' settlements, but instead to display their bravery. European military tactics, therefore, were of little interest to Champlain's allies, whose goal was to kill or capture as many Iroquois as possible. Champlain also did not appreciate that Huron warriors felt no obligation to obey the demands of a war leader unless they respected him and his plans. Totally unaware of his own contribution to the outcome, Champlain recalled the engagement bitterly in his 1632 memoirs,* Voyages to New France.

"At three o'clock in the afternoon, we arrived before the fort of [the Huron and Algonkians'] enemies, where the savages made some skirmishes with each other, although our design was not to disclose ourselves until the next day, which however the impatience of our savages would not permit, both on account of their desire to see fire opened upon their enemies, and also that they might rescue some of their own men who had become too closely engaged, and were hotly pressed. Then I approached the enemy, and although I had only a few men, yet we showed them what they had never seen nor heard before; for, as soon as they saw us and heard the arquebus [musket] shots and the balls whizzing in their ears, they withdrew speedily to their fort, carrying the dead and wounded in this charge. We also withdrew to our main body, with five or six wounded, one of whom died.

"This done, we withdrew to the distance of cannon range, out of sight of the enemy, but contrary to my advice and to what they had promised me. This moved me to address them very rough and angry words in order to incite them to do their duty, foreseeing that if everything should go according to their whim and the guidance of their council, their utter ruin would be the result. Nevertheless I did not fail to send to them and propose means which they should use in order to get possession of their enemies.

*An illustration of the battle of 1615, published in 1632 in Samuel de Champlain's memoirs,* Voyages to New France.

"These were, to make with certain kinds of wood a *cavalier* [an elevated, enclosed wooden platform] which would be higher than the palisades. Upon this were to be placed four or five of our arquebusiers, who should keep up a constant fire over their palisades and galleries, which were well provided with stones, and by this means dislodge the enemy who might attack us from their galleries. . . . This proposition they thought good and very seasonable, and immediately proceeded to carry them out as I directed.

"[The next day] we approached to attack the village, our cavalier being carried by two hundred of the strongest men, who put it down before the village at a pike's length off. I ordered three arquebusiers to mount upon it, who were well protected from the arrows and stones that could be shot or hurled at them. Meanwhile the enemy did not fail to send a large number of arrows which did not miss, and a great many stones, which they hurled from their palisades. Nevertheless a hot fire of arquebusiers forced them to dislodge and abandon their galleries, in consequence of the cavalier which uncovered them, they not venturing to show themselves, but fighting under shelter. Now when the cavalier was carried forward, instead of bringing up the mantelets [large wooden shields] according to order, including . . . one under cover of which we were to set [a] fire, they abandoned them and began to scream at their enemies, shooting arrows into the fort, which in my opinion did little harm to the enemy.

"But we must excuse them, for they are not warriors, and besides will have no discipline nor correction, and will do only what they please. Accordingly one of them set fire inconsiderately to the wood placed against the fort of the enemy, quite the wrong way and in the face of the wind, so that it produced no effect.

"This fire being out, the greater part of the savages began to carry wood against the palisades, but in so small quantity that the fire could have no great effect. There also arose such disorder among them that one could not understand another, which greatly troubled me. In vain did I shout in their ears and remonstrate to my utmost with them as to the danger to which they exposed themselves by their bad behavior, but on account of the great noise they made they heard nothing. Seeing that shouting would only burst my head, and that my remonstrances were useless for putting a stop to the disorder, I did nothing more, but determined together with my men to do what we could, and fire upon such as we could see. . . .

"We were engaged in this combat about three hours, in which two of our chiefs and leading warriors were wounded, namely, one called Ochateguain and another Orani, together with some fifteen common warriors. The others, seeing their men and some of the chiefs wounded, now began to talk of a retreat without farther fighting, in expectation of the five hundred men, whose arrival could not be much delayed. Thus they retreated, a disorderly rabble.

"Moreover the chiefs have in fact no absolute control over their men, who are governed by their own will and follow their own fancy, which is the cause of their disorder and the ruin of all their undertakings; for, having determined upon anything with their leaders, it needs only the whim of a villain, or nothing at all, to lead them to break it off and form a new plan. Thus there is no concert of action among them, as can be seen by this expedition."

(continued from page 44)

Whenever we had to go from one village to another for some necessity or business we used to go freely to their dwellings to lodge and get our food, and they received us in them and treated us very kindly although they were under no obligation to us. For they hold it proper to help wayfarers and to receive among them with politeness anyone who is not an enemy, and much more so those of their own nation. They reciprocate hospitality and give such assistance to one another that the necessities of all are provided for without there being any indigent beggar in their towns and villages; and they considered it a very bad thing when they heard it said that there were in France a great many of these needy beggars, and thought that this was for lack of charity in us, and blamed us for it severely.

Aside from their customary friendliness to visitors, the Huron's treatment of the missionaries was motivated by their view of the priests as representatives of France. Champlain himself made an appeal to the Huron to be kind to the priests as a condition of his continuing trade with the Indians.

In the years that followed, trade with the French became more and more important to the Huron. When they had first met Champlain in 1609, the Huron found European products an oddity and a luxury. Within two or three decades, however, these goods, especially metalware, became necessities of a changing way of life. The Huron had so readily accepted new items, such as iron pots, knives, and weapons, into their culture that people gradually lost the skills needed to make this equipment using their traditional methods and materials. Within only two or three generations after the Huron's introduction to European goods, no one among them remembered how to manufacture their own wood or stone utensils.

Because of the Huron's dependence on outside sources for these necessary products, the fur trade became the mainstay of the Huron economy. As the Huron wanted more of these goods, they had to obtain more beaver pelts to trade with the French. Soon the beaver virtually disappeared in Huronia owing to this heavy trapping. By 1630 the Huron could get pelts only by trading for them with other tribes. Luckily, the Huron could rely on their traditional Algonkian trading partners for a steady supply of pelts. In exchange, the Huron offered corn and beans, which they continued to grow. This produce was always needed by the Algonkians, especially by the Nipissing, who could not farm enough for themselves during the short growing season in their cold climate. To maintain this three-way system of exchange, Huron men had to spend more time on trading expeditions to visit both the Algonkian suppliers of beaver pelts and French suppliers of manufactured goods. Huron women as well had to work harder planting and tending larger fields than they had in the past in order to have enough surplus produce for trading purposes. In

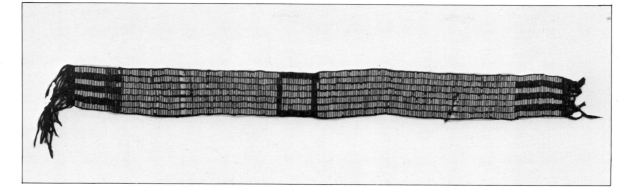

*A wampum belt given to the Iroquois Nation by the Huron to commemorate the signing of a peace treaty in 1612. This was one of many unsuccessful attempts in the early 17th century to end the fighting between the confederacies. The dark square in the center represents the Huron; the dark stripes, people; and the white stripes, peace. The message contained in the belt is "The people of both nations walk in peace together."*

this way, both men and women were involved in supplying the necessary ingredients for the Huron's success in their intensified trade economy.

The Huron's position as middlemen in the fur trade was soon threatened by the Iroquois. In about 1610 the Dutch had begun traveling north along the Hudson River and following the Mohawk River inland. Here, just south of Huron and Algonkian territory in what is now upstate New York, the Dutch entered into trade relationships with a number of Indian groups, including the Iroquois. Soon the Iroquois had trapped most of the relatively small beaver population in their territory and were forced, as the Huron had been, to initiate trade with Indians farther north to obtain pelts. But both the Huron and the Iroquois wanted these tribes to trade only with them. As each of these two powerful confederacies tried to expand the area of its own influence, direct conflict between them increased.

Initially, the manufactured goods that the Indians obtained from Europeans made their daily lives easier. During the course of several decades, however, their dependence on these products engulfed all of the tribes in what is now the northeastern United States in competition and conflict that proved deadly to their traditional ways of life. The Huron's culture would be especially threatened in the years that followed by two adversaries, one old and one new. The old enemy was the Iroquois, who would become increasingly aggressive in their attempts to destroy their trading competitors. The new adversary would be French missionaries. These men would attack the Huron in a more subtle but nearly as devastating way as they pressured the Indians to abandon their traditions.

*A 19th-century engraving of Jesuit priest Jean de Brébeuf preaching Christianity to a gathering of Indians.*

# THE
# CRITICAL
# YEARS

The 15 years between 1634 and 1649 were a time of intense change and turmoil for the Huron. At the beginning of this brief period, French priests of the Jesuit order established the first missions among the Huron. Directly and indirectly, this event would have a major influence on the history of the Huron people.

Since 1615, when Father LeCaron had first visited the Huron, Recollet and Jesuit priests had occasionally made trips to Huronia. They traveled from village to village and some began to learn the Huron language during these visits so that they could communicate with the Indians in their native tongue. Few, however, stayed among the Huron for long.

The work of French missionaries in New France, as Canada was then known in Europe, was interrupted in 1629 when an expedition of British soldiers forced Champlain to surrender Quebec. The French priests were forced to leave the region, but many Jesuits returned in 1632, when France regained

control of the post. The first new missions were established in 1634 under the leadership of Jesuit Father Jean de Brébeuf. The same year de Brébeuf traveled to several villages in Huronia, where he was greeted by the Huron with their customary hospitality. Encouraged by his reception, other Jesuits soon followed and set up missions in several Huron villages in 1635. From that time onward, French priests and lay workers at the missions became familiar to the Huron and began to have a great effect over the Indians' daily lives.

Most of the Huron's interest in the priests was limited to the unfamiliar manufactured articles they brought with them from Europe. For instance, one missionary reported that some Huron were fascinated by a clock he owned that made a noise as it struck each hour. The Huron interpreted the noise as a sign that the clock possessed supernatural power. The Huron were also impressed with the Jesuits' ability to read and write. Many wanted to learn these skills so they could send written messages to relatives and friends in other villages.

The unusual talents and property of the priests helped them to exert influence over the Indians. Curious about the way the priests lived or eager to borrow their tools, Huron often visited them in their cabins, which the missionaries usually built on the outskirts of the Indians' settlements. The Jesuits took advantage of these opportunities to talk to the Huron about Christianity. In this informal setting, they hoped to start the process that would lead to the Indians' conversion. Most Huron showed no interest in the priests' teachings, but some listened politely, and a small number even attended Catholic masses conducted by the fathers.

In addition to converting the Indians, the Jesuits hoped to persuade them to end certain traditional social practices. The priests understood that religious beliefs are related to other elements of culture; therefore, they knew that they would need to persuade the Huron to adopt other European beliefs and customs to convert them successfully.

The missionaries especially hoped to change the Huron's attitudes about personal freedom. Because the Huron believed that all people have the right to make decisions for themselves, they did not recognize outside authorities as having the power to make people obey or conform to a certain mode of behavior. These beliefs contrasted sharply with those of most Europeans, including the Jesuits. European political and religious leaders had tremendous authority. People were expected to follow the rulings of government officials and to accept the teachings of priests on faith and without question. Even in European families, the power of parents, especially fathers, over their children and of husbands over their wives was not to be challenged.

The priests were particularly critical of Huron marriage practices. The Indians believed that when a woman and a man liked each other and wanted to live together they could do so. They also believed that if a couple no longer cared to stay together, or if they argued continually, they could separate and look for other partners. These practices were an extension of the Huron's attitudes about personal freedom, but they seemed blasphemous to Europeans, who believed that no matter what happened in a marriage, a couple should stay together. The missionaries succeeded in convincing some Huron who converted to adopt these attitudes, but they were a very small minority. In fact, many Huron rejected Christianity precisely because of the Jesuits' insistence on lifelong marriage. Most Huron thought that the few converts' behavior was odd, and many saw it as a betrayal of their traditional values.

The way the Huron reared their children caused similar problems for the missionaries. Huron parents did not assert authority over their offspring. If children misbehaved, adults patiently corrected them but never threatened

*An engraving from 1664 of an Iroquoian Indian family. The missionaries who lived among the Huron believed they should be less indulgent in raising their children.*

them. The French, in contrast, condoned harsh punishments for children. Huron who visited Quebec were shocked to see French parents scolding or beating their offspring. This behavior was so repulsive to the Indians that the Jesuits' instruction to the Huron on child rearing was never successful, even among converts.

The Huron and the Jesuits also had conflicting attitudes about how criminals should be punished. Among the Huron, the family of the offender shared responsibility for a crime. For instance, if someone injured another person, the attacker and his or her family atoned for the act by presenting gifts to the victim's relatives. For serious offenses, such as murder, the killer's relatives had to offer a specific number of gifts, usually belts made of shell beads, known as wampum. Even if the murderer disappeared, his or her family was expected to deliver these goods.

The Jesuits wanted the Huron to abandon this practice, which they thought allowed a criminal to escape direct punishment, and recommended that the Indians instead publicly beat wrongdoers, as people did in France. However, the priests failed to realize that the public dishonor and financial burden undertaken by a criminal's family to make amends were in fact very strong deterrents to crime. Even the Jesuits admitted that crime was extremely rare in Huron society. Father Gabriel Lalemant wrote in 1645 that "in those practices which among [the Huron] are regarded as evil acts and are condemned by the public, we find without comparison much less disorder than there is in France, though here the mere shame of having committed the crime is the offender's punishment."

The Jesuits also opposed the Huron's use of dream analysis and belief that dreams expressed hidden desires that needed to be fulfilled to maintain good health. The priests' ridicule of the Ononharoia, the Huron's dream-guessing ritual, led many Indians to reject

Christianity. The Huron resented the assault on this treasured ritual, as they feared the loss of all of the traditions that united Huron society, comforted individuals, and gave meaning to their lives.

The unconverted Huron's suspicion and dislike of the French priests grew when a series of smallpox and measles epidemics spread throughout Huronia between 1635 and 1640. These diseases were caused by germs that had not existed in North America before European contact. Because American Indians had never been exposed to these germs, they had not developed immunities to them. They therefore readily caught these viruses, which usually proved to be fatal.

Smallpox and measles germs were transmitted to the Huron both when they traveled and in their own villages. When Huron men went to Quebec to trade furs, they came in contact with French people who were ill with these diseases or who appeared well but were germ carriers. The Huron traders often caught these harmful viruses and brought them back to their villages in Huronia. Some missionaries and lay mission workers were also carriers of disease. As they traveled and lived among the Huron, they unwittingly transmitted these viruses to the Indian people.

A short time after the Huron's initial exposure, smallpox and measles devastated their population. In 1634 there were 20,000 Indians living in Huronia;

*The frontispiece of* Long Journey to the Country of the Huron, *Recollet priest Gabriel Theodat de Sagard's account of his experiences during a visit to* Huronia *in 1623. The book was annotated and published as part of Sagard's* History of Canada *in 1636. The priest hoped the book would encourage the French government to rescind its 1632 order forbidding the Recollets from traveling to North America.*

by 1640, only 10,000 were left. This disaster had many effects on Huron society. The extensive illness and many deaths caused great confusion, bitterness, and sorrow among the people. Every Huron mourned the death of loved ones. Often entire families died from disease. The Huron suffered the loss of respected leaders and people with important skills. Also, young children died in huge numbers, creating potential economic catastrophe because in the future there would be few adults to perform vital activities, such as farming and trading.

To the Huron perhaps the most horrifying aspect of the epidemics was their ignorance of the diseases' cause. American Indians had never experienced viruses that resulted in such widespread death. Terrified by the epidemics' power, they turned to their traditional healers for cures. Native methods of healing, however, had no effect on smallpox and measles.

The Huron then sought an explanation for the epidemics by studying the pattern of the spread of these diseases. People accurately observed that they had been unknown among them before the arrival of the French. The Huron also noticed that the families that had the most frequent contact with missionaries experienced the greatest number of deaths. They therefore concluded that the French were directly responsible for the epidemics.

The Huron were absolutely correct, but they misunderstood the method of contagion. No one in the 17th century, either Indian or European, knew that diseases spread through germs. The Huron instead blamed the epidemics on spells cast by the Jesuits, a deduction that was consistent with their belief that some evil human beings had supernatural powers that they could use to harm others. The priests tried to dismiss such claims, but because they, too, knew nothing of how disease spread, they could not offer the Huron a better explanation for the sudden and severe epidemics. Father Gabriel Lalemant, writing in 1640, presented a deeply disturbing image of these times:

No doubt, they said, it must needs be that we had a secret understanding with the disease (for they believe that it is a demon), since we alone were all full of life and health, although we constantly breathed nothing but a totally infected air. Wherein truly it must be acknowledged that these poor people are in some sense excusable. For it has happened very often, that where we were most welcome, where we baptized most people, there it was in fact where they died the most; and, on the contrary, in the cabins to which we were denied entrance, although they were sometimes sick to extremity, at the end of a few days one saw every person prosperously cured. We shall see in heaven the secret, but ever adorable, judgments of God therein.

The Huron's suspicions led many to want to expel the priests from Huronia.

But the missionaries were protected for two reasons. By the early 1640s, the Jesuits had been able to convert a small number of influential people in the tribes. Some converts were leaders of clans and large families and able to use their positions to persuade the people in their villages not to act against the priests. The Huron also still depended on trade with the French for many of the manufactured goods they needed and desired. To maintain friendly relations with French traders, they had to allow the Jesuits to stay among them.

Gradually, factions arose in Huron villages that either supported or opposed the presence of the priests. Most supporters were people who had converted to Christianity for one of a variety of reasons. Some did so because they were impressed by the Jesuits' technological knowledge and equipment. Others were motivated by the economic benefits the French granted to converts. French merchants in Quebec gave Christian Indians better rates of exchange, so converts could receive more goods for the same number of furs than Indians who held on to their traditional beliefs. Some Huron converted after 1641, when the French government ruled that their people could trade guns to Indians, but only to Indians who were Christian.

The Jesuits were also able to persuade many dying Huron to be baptized during the epidemics by convincing them that they would not join their relatives after death unless they converted. Father Joseph Le-Mercier noted in his journal, however, that the Christian view of the afterworld did not appeal to every Huron: "[One] told us that he thought it was wrong that they should not work in heaven, that it was not well to be idle; and for this reason he had no desire to go there." Despite the Huron's increasing acceptance of Christianity, the majority retained their traditional beliefs. Their own religion gave them an understanding of the world and their place in it that the Europeans' Catholicism did not.

The traditional Huron began to ridicule the converts for refusing to participate in old customs, especially in rituals of curing and thanksgiving. As the Huron's hostility grew, the Jesuits decided to build a separate mission village, which they named Sainte-Marie, on the banks of the Wye River. There in 1639 they erected several European-style log cabins, a church, and a hospital. Some Huron converts came to live in Sainte-Marie and built their own longhouses there. This small community served as a permanent mission and as the setting for Christian Hurons' celebrations of Catholic holidays.

At the same time that pressures from missionaries threatened to destroy the unity of the Huron people, they also came under increased attacks from the Iroquois that would soon prove even more devastating to their way of life. In the early 1640s, the Iroquois' desire to control trade along the St. Lawrence

*A modern reconstruction of the 17th-century Jesuit mission at Sainte-Marie. Some of the original stonework survives.*

River grew more desperate. As the Huron had become increasingly dependent on trade with Europeans, so had the Iroquois. They, too, had overhunted the beaver in their homelands and now sought to take the beaver hunted by the northern tribes. The Mohawk already controlled trade along the Hudson River leading to the Dutch post at Fort Orange (later Albany), and they had designs on the French trade as well. To keep northern Indians from transporting their furs to the French trading posts, Mohawk warriors set up am-

bushes along the river and its tributaries and in the surrounding forests. They attacked Indian traders from many tribes who traveled through this area en route to Quebec and tried to steal their goods. Sometimes Huron traders evaded these ambushes or overcame the Iroquois. But they were defeated often enough to arouse great fear among Huron men, many of whom soon refused to take part in trading expeditions.

Some Huron chiefs tried to make alliances with the Iroquois in order to put

*The martyrdom of Jesuit priests Jean de Brébeuf and Gabriel Lalemant during the Iroquois' attack on their mission village in 1649. The Iroquois inflicted such tortures on the missionaries as pouring boiling water over their heads in a mockery of baptism.*

an end to the fighting. However, these peace efforts were not successful. During negotiations, there were usually fewer attacks, but these lulls never lasted for long. Over time, the Huron's casualties increased and their panic grew.

After 1642 the Iroquois developed a new, more deadly pattern of warfare against the Huron. Warriors from the westernmost Iroquois nations, particularly the Seneca, who lived closest to

Huronia, began invading Huron villages. The victims of these attacks were most often people traveling along the paths that linked settlements, and women working in the fields. Soon Huron women were so afraid of the Iroquois that they would not plant or harvest crops. The resulting food shortages further weakened the Huron.

In 1648 the Iroquois launched a campaign aimed at the total defeat of the Huron Confederacy. Armed with guns they had obtained from the Dutch, large groups of Iroquois warriors invaded Huronia and destroyed the villages in their path. As each village was attacked, the inhabitants who were able to escape fled to other settlements for temporary shelter. But eventually there was no place in Huronia that was safe from the Iroquois.

This warfare took a tremendous toll on the Huron. Many were killed in the Iroquois' attacks, further reducing their disease-ravaged population. Shortages of food resulted in mass starvation. Renewed epidemics also spread among the people already weakened by hunger and fear. By the end of 1649 the Huron felt they had no choice but to abandon their homeland and therefore disband the Huron Confederacy.

Reasoning that they would be safe from the Iroquois only if they became Iroquois, some Huron relocated in the Iroquois Nations. Following Iroquoian tradition, the Iroquois were willing to incorporate their Huron enemies into their tribes in order to replenish their population, which had decreased over years of steady warfare. Approximately 1,000 settled among the Onondaga, who adopted the refugees into their families and villages. Others, including most of the Tahontaenrat, joined the Seneca, who offered the Huron their own village, which was named Gandougarae (gan-DO-ga-ray). Many of the Huron who agreed to move to Seneca territory wanted to be reunited with family members who had been captured by the Seneca during warfare. Converted Huron were encouraged to move to Gandougarae by the Seneca's assurance that they would be allowed to practice Christianity, despite the Iroquois's usual hostility toward European religion and missionaries.

Most Huron refused to merge with the Iroquois. One group chose instead to travel southwest and settle among their Algonquian-speaking Indian neighbors and trading partners, the Neutrals and the Petun. Others sought safety on the island of Gahoendoe (now Christian Island) in Georgian Bay. Both havens, however, proved only temporary. For decades, these small contingents of Huron would be forced to move from place to place to find land or to escape conflict with stronger enemies. The end of the Huron Confederacy, therefore, marked the beginning of a displaced and divided people. ▲

*A 17th-century engraving of a fortified house at Quebec, after a drawing by Champlain.*

## FROM
# HURONIA
## TO
# LORETTE

The Huron who traveled to the island of Gahoendoe in 1649 to escape Iroquois attacks hoped that they had found a safe refuge. Within a year, however, disaster struck them there, too. Farmland on Gahoendoe was scarce. Although the Huron had been able to bring some ripened corn to the island when they escaped from Huronia, they soon suffered from food shortages. To survive, small groups returned to the mainland to collect wild foods, such as acorns and berries, on familiar terrain. These food-gathering expeditions were frequently attacked by Iroquois warriors who were still roaming through Huronia. Many people were killed, and those who remained on Gahoendoe grew terrified.

By the winter, the Huron were starving. Weakened by lack of food, many succumbed to renewed outbreaks of smallpox. Because most of the Gahoendoe Huron were Christians, several Jesuits had come with them to the island. These priests encouraged the Huron to escape these horrible conditions and to seek a new life as far away as possible. The Huron agreed, and together with the fathers they made plans to travel east.

On June 10, 1650, approximately 300 Huron left the lands of their ancestors and set out for Quebec. As they neared the French town of Montreal, they met a group of Huron and French soldiers. These travelers were bringing supplies of food and arms from Quebec to embattled Huronia. When they learned that the Huron had abandoned their homeland, this relief expedition joined the Gahoendoe contingent, and all soon proceeded northeast along the St. Lawrence River. The Huron wished to leave Montreal as quickly as possible because the town was just across the river from the lands of their Mohawk enemies.

Approximately 400 Huron arrived at Quebec on July 28, 1650. With no claim to land in the area, they had to rely on French individuals and the Catholic

# EASTERN HURON SETTLEMENTS, 1650–PRESENT

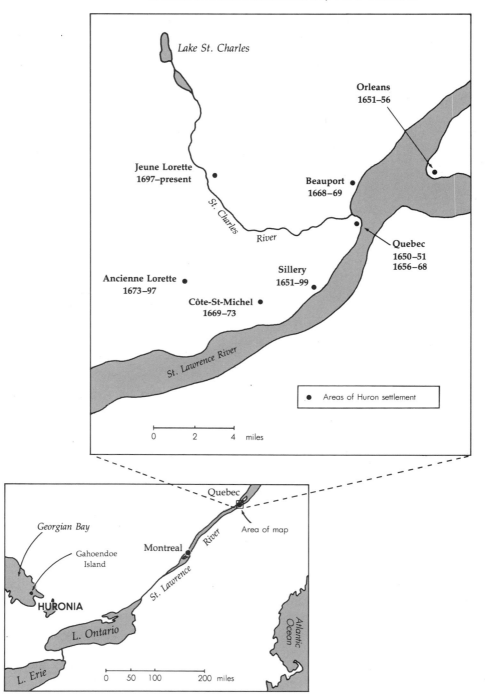

*Lake St. Charles*

Orleans
1651–56

Jeune Lorette
1697–present

Beauport
1668–69

*St. Charles River*

Quebec
1650–51
1656–68

Ancienne Lorette
1673–97

Sillery
1651–99

Côte-St-Michel
1669–73

*St. Lawrence River*

● Areas of Huron settlement

0   2   4   miles

Quebec

*Georgian Bay*

Gahoendoe
Island

Montreal

*St. Lawrence River*

Area of map

HURONIA

*Atlantic Ocean*

L. Ontario

L. Erie

0   50   100   200   miles

church to donate enough for their needs. On this territory, the Huron continued to plant fields and to fish and hunt in their traditional manner. Partly because immigrants arrived from other areas and partly because of a natural increase in births, their population soon grew.

In 1651 the Huron left Quebec to explore the surrounding area. Eventually they relocated on Orleans, an island in the St. Lawrence River. At this new settlement, their population grew to between 500 and 600 because many Indians from other missions came to live among them. The Huron remained at Orleans until 1656, when Mohawk warriors made a surprise attack on them as they were working in their fields. The Mohawk killed about 70 people and took others captive. Fearing for their lives, in July 1656 the Huron who were able to escape decided to leave Orleans and again seek safety near the fortified town of Quebec.

After the attack on Orleans, the Huron realized that the only way to ensure their own security was to negotiate a lasting peace with the Iroquois, especially with their Mohawk enemies. The Mohawk agreed to send a delegation to Quebec to discuss the matter with the Huron leaders. The Mohawk delegates were willing to negotiate a peace treaty but insisted as a condition that the Huron agree to move to Mohawk territory and live in their villages. The Mohawk had lost many men in constant warfare and, like the Huron, had been victims of smallpox and measles epidemics.

They hoped to replenish their population with Huron immigrants. Seeing no alternative, the Huron reluctantly agreed to join the Mohawk.

In the spring of 1657, the Mohawk delegation and a group of Onondaga arrived at Quebec to lead the Huron back to Iroquois territory. But some Huron had changed their minds about joining them. Among themselves, the Huron debated the issue again, and each tribe came to a different decision about its future. The Arendahronon chose to join the Onondaga, the Attignawantan left with the Mohawk, and the Attigneenongnahac decided to stay in Quebec. Soon after leaving Quebec the Arendahronon were betrayed by their Onondaga guides. Their men were killed, and the women were taken as captives. However, the Huron who decided to live among the Mohawks arrived in their new villages safely and were adopted into Mohawk families. At first these people retained their own language and customs. But as years passed and the Huron developed friendships with and married Mohawk, they gradually adopted the ways of the Iroquois.

After decades of conflict, the Iroquois and the French at last concluded a peace in 1667. Only then did the Huron who had remained in Quebec feel secure enough to travel outside of the fortified town to their fields and hunting areas. A year later, they left the city and took up residence at Beauport, a French town located on the north shore of the St. Lawrence, a few miles down-

*Huron living near Quebec, drawn in the late 18th century.*

river from Quebec. They stayed there until the following year, when they moved several miles south of Quebec to Côte-St-Michel. There the Jesuits had established the mission of Nôtre-Dame-de-Foy, which is today called Sainte-Foy. At that time, the community's population numbered slightly more than 200, but it quickly increased as some Huron who had emigrated west in 1649 and some Christian Iroquois came to live there.

In 1673 the Huron left Sainte-Foy and moved a short distance west to the mission site at Ancienne Lorette (Old Lorette) to accommodate their growing population, which was then about 300. The Huron remained there for 24 years. In 1697 their increasing numbers led them to make their final migration. They traveled to an area about eight miles north of Quebec and established a settlement there near a Jesuit mission named Jeune Lorette (Young Lorette). After decades of moving from place to place, this branch of the Huron at last had found a permanent home.

The Huron at Jeune Lorette were soon faced with a new problem: In 1701 they lost access to their hunting and

*(continued on page 73)*

# EMBROIDERY IN MOOSEHAIR

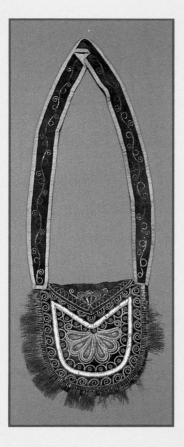

Leather pouch and carrying strap made by Huron in Lorette in about 1830. Both are embroidered with dyed moosehair.

Since the mid-17th century, the Huron in Canada and their non-Indian neighbors have shared many elements of their very different cultures. This interaction is evident in the Huron's beautiful moosehair embroidery, which weds European decorative designs with Indian materials.

Huron moosehair embroidery dates from 1639, when five French nuns established a seminary in Quebec for young Indian girls. The sisters taught their students, including many Huron, to embroider with French thread. When the nuns had exhausted their supply of European materials, they began to use moosehair instead, possibly at the suggestion of their pupils. The Indians of eastern North America had long employed moosehair, dyed brilliant colors with pigments made from plants, to decorate objects they made.

Because individual shafts of moosehair are too short to stay in place when threaded through cloth or skin, the nuns and their students developed a new embroidery technique—appliqué. By creating shapes with bunches of hair shafts and then sewing them onto pelts with sinew, Huron embroiderers adorned moccasins, coats, and other leather goods.

By the early 19th century, the Huron in Canada had developed their embroidering talents into an industry. Men in workshops cut leather into small pieces that women then embroidered and assembled into clothing in their homes. As the demand for these goods increased, the Huron began to make their decorations less intricate and thus less time-consuming to produce. Although some Huron continue to embroider using old methods and materials, most moccasins made today on the Huron reserve are unadorned or decorated with simple beadwork patterns.

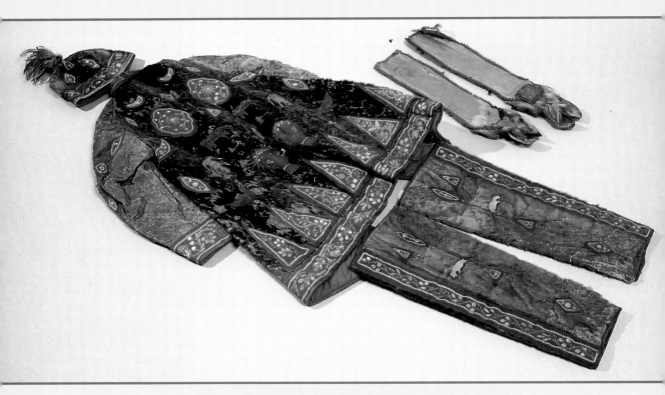

The back (above) and front (below) of a sealskin hat, coat, and leggings, made in about 1780. This suit, which was probably owned by a Huron chief, is decorated with embroidered red cloth panels sewn to the skin. The human heads and animals on the back of the coat and the front of the leggings represent characters in a traditional Huron story.

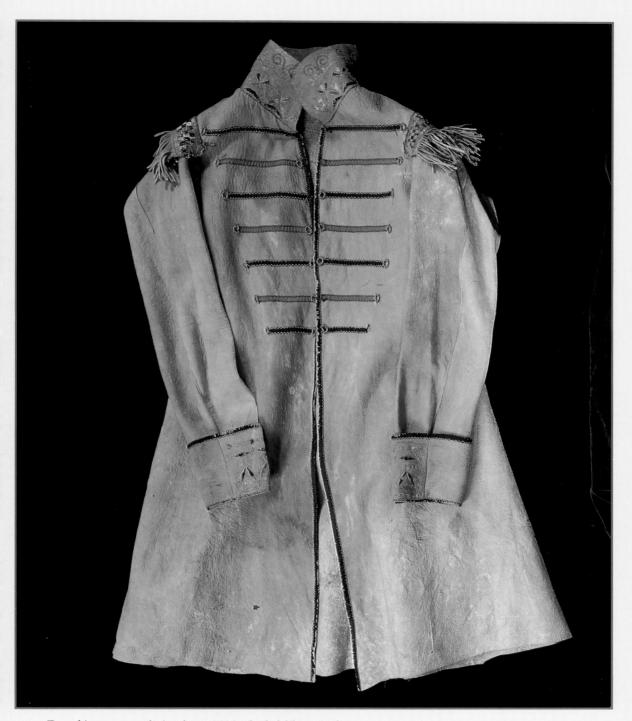

*Deerskin coat, made in about 1839. Styled like a 19th-century European army officer's coat, this garment is embroidered at the collar and cuffs with porcupine quills, a material particularly popular with Iroquois artisans.*

*Wool tablecloth, 6′ x 5′8′′, made in about 1860. This item is constructed from three layers of cloth sewn together at the sides with silk ribbon. The embroidered upper piece is backed with a thin piece of birchbark to hold in place the strands of moosehair that have been threaded through the cloth. Each stitch was made with a single strand of hair.*

*Above: Embroidered cloth and birch-bark novelty, 2½" wide, made in 1850. The Huron sewed trinkets such as this for sale in Europe.*

*Right: Cloth eyeglass case embroidered with moosehair appliqué, made in 1840.*

*Embroidered birch-bark container, 4" x 2½", made in about 1850. The Huron's decorative boxes, which they often embroidered with brown and green moosehair, were greatly valued by European traders.*

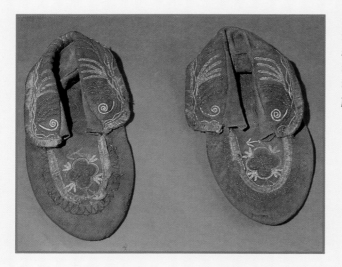

*Embroidered moccasins, each 10″ long, made in the late 1800s. The relative simplicity of the design on these shoes is typical of the embroidery produced by the Huron workshops during this period.*

Below and right: *Pairs of tanned leather moccasins, each shoe 10½″ long, made in about 1840. The Huron often dyed skins black to create a contrast with their multicolored moosehair appliqué.*

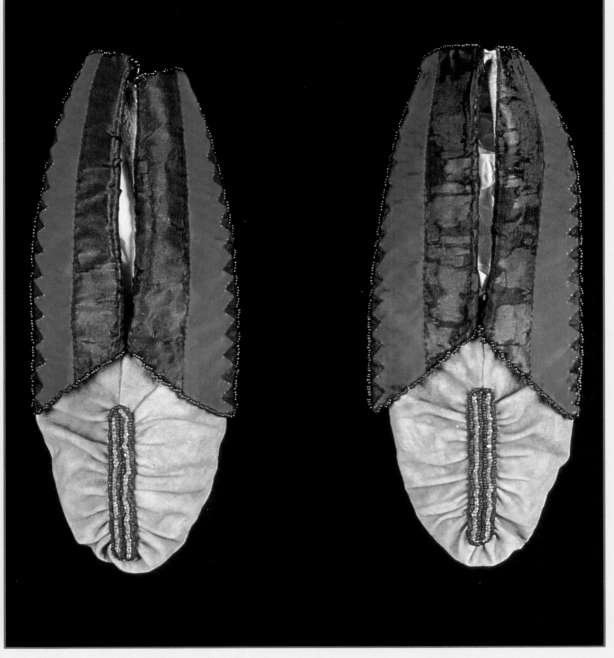

*Women's leather moccasins, each 9½" long, made in 1912. Decorated with rows of beads and red tafetta ankle flaps, these shoes were crafted by Maggie Coon, a Wyandot woman, for wear during summer festivals. Unlike the Huron in Lorette, the Wyandot did not manufacture moccasins for sale.*

*Tanned leather moccasins, each 10'' long, made in about 1780. Constructed by Huron in Detroit, this pair is decorated with dyed porcupine quills and glass beads.*

*Deerskin moccasin, 10'' long, made in about 1840. The shoe is adorned with leather fringe and a variety of items the Huron obtained through trade: tubular glass beads made to imitate wampum (Indian shell beads); globular glass ornaments known as pony beads; and small pieces of tin.*

*Wampum belts displayed in Chartres Cathedral in France. The lower one was made by Christian Huron in Ancienne Lorette and sent to Chartres in 1678. The Latin phrase on this belt reads, "Offering of the Huron to the Virgin with child."*

(continued from page 64)

fishing territory located a few miles south of Quebec near a mission at Sillery. The Jesuits had founded this mission in 1635 and had established there a boarding school for Indian children. Over the years, the priests had persuaded a small number of Huron families to send their offspring to the school for instruction. In 1651 the Company of New France, a private trading firm that owned the surrounding land, had offered this region to Christian Huron to attract their trade and to entice other Huron to convert. The French government ratified this land transaction a few months later in the Act of Concession of 1651. But throughout the late 17th century, the size of the territory allocated to the Huron at Sillery diminished as various neighboring landowners disputed the Company of New France's claim to the area. In 1699 the French government ruled that the Huron no longer had the right to use any of this land. The Huron's repeated appeals for the return of Sillery were denied.

During the early years of the 18th century, the Huron tried to maintain their traditional way of life as much as possible. They continued to plant their fields with corn and beans and also began to grow some grains, such as wheat and rye, that were introduced to North America by Europeans. But the soil at Jeune Lorette was too sandy to farm productively. The Huron, therefore, had to rely more and more on trading animal pelts and lumber from the surrounding forests to the French in nearby Quebec in exchange for produce. As they frequented the growing town, the Huron became more familiar with European life.

Toward the end of the 18th century, the Huron people began to manufacture various goods, such as moccasins, snowshoes, and canoes, that could be traded or sold in Quebec for much more profit than the skins and wood used to make them. The several small workshops the Huron set up in Jeune Lorette employed mainly men, but women helped to manufacture moccasins by embroidering them with dyed moosehair and porcupine quills. The women also made for sale other decorated clothing, such as collars and caps, and baskets woven from the birch bark and sweet grass that they gathered nearby.

When the Huron first began these industries, they still engaged in some farming and hunting. They were encouraged to continue these traditional activities in 1772 when the British gave

*A view of Quebec in 1733. The proximity of the Huron villages at Lorette to this growing town brought the Indians in close contact with European settlers and traders.*

*Huron men making snowshoes at a Lorette workshop, photographed in the early 20th century.*

them 1,352 acres of land approximately 2 miles west of Jeune Lorrette known as Quarante Arpents, meaning "40 arpents." (An arpent is a French unit of land measure.) Since 1763, when the British gained control of New France (which they renamed Canada), the Huron had continually asked the English government for renewed access to the Sillery region. It refused, but recognizing the Huron's need for more territory, it offered them Quarante Arpents instead. A few Huron families farmed

there, but most used it for fishing, hunting, and collecting wood for fuel.

In 1851 the government of Canada granted the Huron a second reserve, a 9,600-acre area called Cabane d'Automne (Autumn Cabin), which was located to the north in the Laurentian mountains. This area was to be used mainly for hunting. But by this time hunting had become much less important to the Huron. Manufacturing was now their major economic activity, as they had begun to sell the products they

*A 1910 photograph of a Huron chief and his grandson in ceremonial clothing. Clan leaders were revered by the tribe even after the Canadian government had taken away their political power.*

made at Lorette in cities throughout Canada and the northeastern United States. Instead of making use of the land at Cabane d'Automne themselves, the Huron allowed Canadian officials to negotiate leases of some of the forests in the area to non–Indian-owned lumber companies, which paid rent to the Huron community.

Like the Huron's traditional economy, the Indians' culture changed in response to their increased contact with Canadian society. By the middle of the 18th century, the Huron had given up their communal longhouses in favor of European-style family dwellings. This change reflected the gradual breakdown of the traditional kinship system based on clan membership. By this time clans no longer owned land or houses. Political leadership came from the national government, and real power had gradually been taken away from the Huron communities and their clan elders. Although the Huron people resisted many of these changes, they did not have the political or economic authority to prevent them. Huron clans continued to have some symbolic functions, but they, too, decreased as more Huron gave up their traditional beliefs and converted to Catholicism.

As the interaction between the growing populations of the Huron and of the nearby Canadian communities increased, the Indians and non-Indians became more familiar with each other on a personal basis. Work and social associations led over time to the intermarriage of Huron and French Canadians, which in turn created a further blending of cultures. Soon almost all Huron spoke French, and fewer and fewer remembered the Huron language.

By the end of the 19th century, the Huron in Canada had all but abandoned their traditional occupations. So few families made use of their lands at Cabane d'Automne and Quarante Arpents, in fact, that the Huron decided to sell these reserves in 1903 and 1904, respectively. As the new century began, the people who remained on the reservation at Lorette continued to identify themselves as Huron. Their way of life, however, came increasingly to resemble that of the non-Indian Canadians in nearby Quebec. A symbol of these changing times, the last fluent speaker of Huron died in 1912. ▲

nous ne demandons pas mieux qu'elle soit de Durée
aussy devostre Costé ce qu'il faut pour Cela,

*Des Gens dela Montag*

Vous auez fait assembler icy nostre pere toutes Les
Nations pour faire vn amas de haches et les me
dans la terre, auec la vostre, pour moy qui n'en auo
d'autre, ie me rejouy de ce que vous faites auiourd'huy
J'inuite Les Iroquois a *nous regarder* comme leurs fre

MARINE ET COLONIES
ARCHIVES
COLONIALES

Yenrsiyan
nontague

Toarenguenion, Soueron
Sonnontuan ; p.r les onneiout

Garonhiaren.
Goyogoin.

marque durat
chef des hurons

la brochet
P.r les staouaest durable,

moscoadoue
abenakis dalacadia

*Indian chiefs' signatures on a treaty concluded in Montreal in 1701
establishing peace between the Iroquois and French-allied Indians.
The Huron chief's sign is at left in the second row.*

# 6

# THE HURON
## OF
# THE WEST

The Huron who remained in the east after the exodus from Huronia spent decades searching for a new homeland and then centuries adapting to this location and defending themselves from the enemies they encountered there. The Huron who sought refuge among the Petun in 1649 suffered different but equally arduous ordeals in the years that followed their escape.

Initially these Huron were comfortable and safe in the Petun villages, which were only 26 miles west of Huronia. The Huron's ties to their Petun neighbors had dated from prehistoric times. The ancestors of both groups had lived in southwestern Ontario centuries earlier. Like the Huron, the Petun were Iroquoian in origin and therefore they spoke similar languages and shared basic cultural practices. More recently, the two peoples had continued their association through trade. In exchange for corn and manufactured goods, the Huron obtained tobacco from the Petun, who were sometimes known as the To-

bacco because of their rich harvest of the plant.

The Huron's security in the villages of their trading partners was short-lived, however. At the end of 1649 the Iroquois launched against the Petun a series of attacks as devastating as their earlier campaign in Huronia had been. Fearing total destruction, the Petun and Huron who survived left the Petun homeland and began a long chain of migrations. Their travels would take them first through the Upper Great Lakes region, then into what is now the American Midwest, and finally, two centuries later, to present-day Oklahoma.

During their migrations, the Huron-Petun came into contact with many other Indian groups, some of whom the Huron had already briefly encountered on trading and hunting expeditions. Most were Algonquian-speaking tribes with cultures and languages very different from their own. With some of their new Indian neighbors, the Huron-

Petun would establish trade networks and friendships, but with others they would compete for the resources of the regions they shared.

The first destination of the Huron-Petun was an island called Michilimackinac (me-shil-ee-MAC-ee-nack), an old Algonquian word meaning "place of the big wounded (or lame) person." Located in what is now northern Michigan, north of Lakes Huron and Michigan and south of Lake Superior, this site was desirable because of its excellent fishing, rich land, and easy access by canoe to the settlements of many different Indian trading partners on the mainland. The Huron-Petun built their village close to a settlement of Ottawa Indians who were already living there.

A short time later, the Huron-Petun left Michilimackinac and settled on Huron Island (now called Rock Island) in northwestern Lake Michigan at the entrance of Green Bay. But the Huron-Petun soon learned that Iroquois were staging raids nearby. To evade their enemy, they once again headed west. By

*A 1703 map of Lake Huron. Michilimackinac is in the upper left corner. The excellent fishing in the region led the Huron and many other Indian groups to settle on Michilimackinac in the late 17th century.*

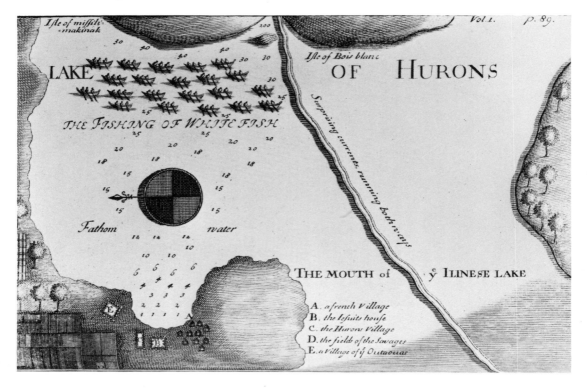

1653 they had relocated along the Black River in what is now northern Wisconsin.

At first this area seemed advantageous. It was rich with fertile land for farming, lakes and rivers for good fishing, and a large population of beavers for trapping. Here the Huron-Petun tried to reestablish the way of life they had known in Huronia. They were especially eager to renew trade relations with Europeans. Since their exodus from their homeland, they had had little contact with French traders and therefore had been unable to obtain the manufactured tools and utensils they needed to replace items that had worn out, broken, or been lost in traveling. In the 1650s and 1660s, Huron-Petun men traveled as far as 800 miles northeast to Quebec in order to trade with French dealers. Some visited their Huron friends who lived near the town, and a few decided to remain among them.

In 1654, after one such expedition, French traders accompanied the Huron-Petun when they returned to the West. These Europeans set up trading posts, first among the Indian groups who still lived at Michilimackinac and later at other villages throughout the Upper Great Lakes region. Thereafter Huron-Petun men could trade with the French at one of these local posts rather than having to make the long and dangerous journey through Iroquois territory to Quebec.

By the late 1650s the Huron-Petun had to contend with a new enemy closer to home. Their settlements along Black River were near the hunting territory of the Sioux Indians, a powerful tribe that lived farther to the west in what are now North and South Dakota. When the Huron-Petun's own hunting and trapping expeditions roamed west, they sometimes encroached upon groups of Sioux, who soon began to threaten and attack them. Once again, the fear of warfare with other Indians forced the Huron-Petun to leave their villages.

In 1661 the Huron-Petun population, which then numbered about 500, migrated north to the southern shore of Lake Superior and built a village in an area known as Chequamegon (che-KWA-me-gon). Chequamegon was a good location for fishing. It also provided opportunities for the Huron-Petun to trade with the other tribes, such as the Ottawa, who already had villages there. The Jesuits had established a mission near these settlements in 1665, but they had little success in converting the Huron-Petun and the other Chequamegon Indians.

The Huron-Petun remained at Chequamegon for a decade, during which they were able to resume trade with the French. Huron-Petun traders became especially active after 1671, when the French and their Indian allies established peace with the Iroquois. They could then safely travel and trade throughout the area without fearing Iroquois attacks. This freedom did not last long, however. By 1670, the Sioux to the west renewed their threats as

*A 19th-century engraving by American artist Frederic Remington depicting an Indian negotiating with a French trader.*

they sought to extend their territory. Now that the Iroquois were their allies, the Huron-Petun decided to go east once again. They returned to their former home near Michilimackinac in 1671 and 1672.

At this time, Michilimackinac was quickly becoming the center for French trade in the entire western Great Lakes region. Indians of many different tribes were drawn there by the abundance of farmland and excellent fishing, as well as the access to French trade goods. Jesuits also came to Michilimackinac and established the mission of St. Ignace nearby, but in this location they still were not able to gain many converts.

The Huron-Petun remained at Michilimackinac until the end of the 17th century. At first they continued to plant crops and reestablish their traditional way of life. During the last years of the century, however, their economy went through a significant change. The Huron-Petun's frequent migrations in the previous decades had disrupted their practice of agriculture. But even in their more permanent Michilimackinac settlements, the Huron-Petun were relying more on fishing, trapping, and especially trading for their livelihood. Agriculture had ceased to be a basic economic activity.

Now, too, their tribal organization and political system began to change. The Huron had traditionally been governed by village, tribal, and Confederacy councils. But the Huron-Petun numbered only 500 and therefore no longer required the complex network of councils that the Huron had needed at the height of the Confederacy to rule their population of 20,000. The Huron-Petun had only local councils, which were less formal than the village councils had been in the past. Clans, however, did remain the basis of social relations, and clan elders still were community leaders.

In the 1680s the British began to compete with the French for control of trade in the Great Lakes region. From the post they established at Albany on the Hudson River, English traders negotiated an alliance with the Iroquois and hoped to extend their influence to other Indians, especially tribes that traded exclusively with their French rivals. This competition between the French and the English led to a disagreement about trading alliances among the Huron-Petun. Some wanted to establish ties with the English, both to obtain English goods and to make their peace with the British-allied Iroquois more secure. Others still distrusted the Iroquois. They wanted instead to strengthen their relations with French traders, who in the past had helped them to defend themselves against Iroquois attacks.

The conflict within the Huron-Petun people temporarily abated when Antoine de Cadillac founded a new post at Detroit in 1701. The French hoped that Detroit's strategic location along the river route between Lake Huron and Lake Erie would help make it the trade center for the entire western Great Lakes region. To protect their interests, the French built a fort there so that they would be prepared for battle if necessary to prevent their English rivals from establishing alliances with northern and western tribes.

Attracted by the intense trading activity at Detroit, the Huron-Petun opted to remain allies of the French. They left Michilimackinac in 1701 and built a village near the new French post. By 1704 several other Indian groups had also established settlements in the area, including the Ottawa and the Potawatomi. At Detroit, these Indians were able to trade for guns and ammunition as well as for household goods and tools.

From their new location, the Huron-Petun began to send hunting expeditions into the region to the south, in what is now northern Ohio near the Sandusky River. There they came into contact with other Indian tribes who lived nearby such as the Lenape, Illinois, and Shawnee. Some of these Indian groups had recently migrated from the east, where their ancestral lands had been encroached upon by Euro-

# HURON-PETUN AND WYANDOT MIGRATIONS, 1650–PRESENT

NORTH DAKOTA

SOUTH DAKOTA

NEBRASKA

KANSAS

MINNESOTA

WISCONSIN

IOWA

MISSOURI

OKLAHOMA

ARKANSAS

TEXAS

MISSISSIPPI

CANADA

L. Superior

Chequamegon

Huron Island

Michilimackinac

L. Huron

MICHIGAN

L. Michigan

HURONIA

L. Ontario

NEW YORK

Detroit

L. Erie

Upper Sandusky

Sandusky

PENNSYLVANIA

OHIO

WEST VIRGINIA

VIRGINIA

INDIANA

ILLINOIS

KENTUCKY

Ohio River

Black River

Mississippi

Missouri River

Neosho River

Arkansas River

1671

1650

1652

1701–4

1658–65

1843

1855–70

Area of inset

Wyandot Reservation

● Areas of Huron-Petun or Wyandot settlement
    Modern state boundaries
    Modern international boundaries

0    50   100          200  miles

## Inset

KANSAS

Quapaw

Peoria

Ottawa

Modoc

Shawnee

WYANDOT

Seneca

Neosho River

Spring River

MISSOURI

*French Jesuit missionary Pierre de Charle-voix praised the Huron's industry and generosity. He wrote, "Were it not for the Hurons the other Indians of [Detroit] must die of hunger."*

pean settlers. The Huron-Petun became allies with some of these Ohio tribes and often provided the most influential leaders in these allegiances. A French explorer and scholar, Pierre de Charlevoix, wrote in his record of his visits to North America in 1721 that "were it not for the Hurons the other Indians of [Detroit] must die of hunger. The Hurons who are wiser, more laborious and more accustomed to husbandry, being also endowed with a greater share of foresight and by means of their indus-

try are in a condition not only to subsist without being beholden to anyone, but also to furnish a supply to their neighbors."

Even after the Huron-Petun moved to Detroit, the English continued to court them as trading partners. In 1745 a Huron chief named Orontony, who had become friendly with the English, moved his followers to a settlement near a British trading post at Sandusky Bay. Two years later, the English encouraged Orontony to attempt to unite several Indian groups against the French. The chief organized an attack on the posts at Detroit, but advance word reached the French and his plan was abandoned. Orontony and more than 100 of his warriors and their families soon left the area and journeyed west into what is now Indiana. In a few years, however, Orontony's influence faded, and these people moved back to Huron-Petun villages near Sandusky and Detroit.

By the mid-18th century, the British were referring to the Huron-Petun by a new name. They called this group the Wyandot, a variation of Wendat, the name the Huron had called themselves before they had contact with European traders.

In the 1750s, competition between the British and the French increased. Although some Wyandot were pro-British, most continued to side with their old allies. They had had long experience with French traders and did not entirely trust the English because of their friendship with the Iroquois. The

Wyandot were also aware that more and more English settlers were moving westward and that they sometimes attacked Indian villages to gain the inhabitants' land.

The tensions between the two European powers broke into full-scale war in North America in 1754 after the French seized the British Fort Pitt at present-day Pittsburgh. British troops led by General Edward Braddock tried to regain the garrison, which the French knew as Fort Duquesne. They were prevented by 300 French soldiers and more than 1,000 warriors from the Wyandot and other French-allied Indian tribes. The French were less successful in subsequent battles in the French and Indian War (1754–63). When they were ultimately defeated, the British forced them to abandon their territorial claims in North America.

Even after France's surrender, its Indian allies continued to battle the British. Led by the great Ottawa chief Pontiac, these Indian forces, which included some Wyandot warriors, waged war on British Detroit and Fort Pitt. The

*A map showing the camps of British and French soldiers near Quebec during the French and Indian War. Following France's defeat at the Battle of the Plains of Abraham on September 13, 1759, Quebec was surrendered to British forces.*

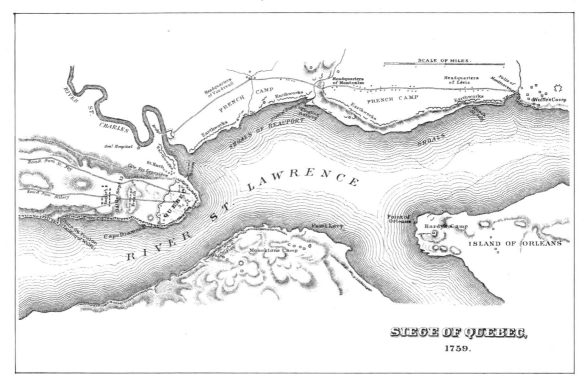

Wyandot also helped Pontiac's Indian army destroy the British fort at Sandusky.

In the end, however, Pontiac's efforts failed to keep the British from establishing power over the Ohio region. Because the defeated French had left North America, the Wyandot had no choice but to begin to trade with the British at Detroit and Sandusky. These trade relations led most Wyandot to side with their former enemies when the American Revolution broke out in 1776. Throughout the war, Wyandot warriors repeatedly attacked American soldiers. In 1782 an American military expedition led by Colonel William Crawford was finally sent to Sandusky to subdue the tribe. To protect their villages, the Wyandot battled the expedition, but the soldiers captured and executed many of their leaders. As the Americans departed, however, the Wyandot were able to retaliate by capturing Colonel Crawford, whom they burned at the stake.

After the American victory over the British in 1783, the Wyandot were faced with the problem of guarding their lands from encroachment by non-Indian settlers from two powerful nations, England and the United States. Although the British lost much of their North American territory according to the terms of the Treaty of Paris, which ended the revolution, they still retained their claim to Canada. Desiring more land for non-Indian Canadians, they soon sought to control the territory occupied by the Wyandot living east of the Detroit River. Simultaneously, the new United States government was eager to secure for its own citizens the prime land the Wyandot occupied near Sandusky and their surrounding hunting territory, which included most of the area that is now Ohio.

Beginning in 1790, the Wyandot were compelled to sign a series of treaties with the British and the American governments. The Wyandot felt threatened by the great military strength of these nations and by the tremendous number of non-Indian settlers moving into their lands. Fearing that all their land would be taken by force if they did not cooperate, the Wyandot consented in each treaty to cede some territory in order to secure legal title to other regions. But officials from both governments often later ignored the promises they had made in these treaties when they wanted more of the Indians' lands.

The Wyandot's first land cession to Britain took place in 1790 under the provisions of the Treaty of Detroit. This agreement gave the British most of the Wyandot's land east of the Detroit River in exchange for a monetary payment and a tract of 23,630 acres north of Lake Erie. The British allowed the Wyandot to retain a mission site near Detroit, however, and also granted them approximately 23,000 acres near the present-day city of Anderdon, Ontario, which they established as a reserve for the exclusive use of the Wyandot. But in subsequent treaties, the British acquired much of the Wyandot's remaining territory: They gained control of the

*A medal given by the U.S. government to Wyandot chief Tarhee at the signing of the Treaty of Greenville in 1795.*

can rivals. After several skirmishes, in 1794 President George Washington sent a force of soldiers led by General Anthony Wayne to defend the area organized as the Northwest Territory (now Ohio, Indiana, Illinois, Michigan, Wisconsin, and part of Minnesota). At Fallen Timbers, an area near present-day Toledo, Ohio, Wayne's troops soundly defeated the warriors of the western Indian confederacy. The Americans were victorious in part because British soldiers failed to join the Indians in the fighting.

As a result of their defeat, the Sandusky Wyandot signed their first agreement with the American government, the Treaty of Greenville, in 1795. Along with several other tribes, including the Illinois, the Shawnee, and the Lenape, they ceded nearly two-thirds of the Indian hunting territory in present-day Ohio.

In 1805 these Indian groups were compelled to cede one-third of their reduced territory; two years later, they relinquished their claims to most of the remaining land. As more white settlers moved into Ohio, the Wyandot feared that it was only a matter of time before they lost their right to the little land they still retained near Sandusky Bay.

During the early years of the 19th century, tensions began to build again between the British and Americans. The United States had become particularly irritated by Britain's refusal to evacuate American territory in the Great Lakes region. These feelings soon erupted into the military conflicts of the

mission land in 1800 and took back two thirds of the Anderdon Reserve in 1836.

The Wyandot at Sandusky were more reluctant than their Canadian kin to negotiate land cessions. Banding with other tribes in the region, they initially resolved to battle the United States in order to hold on to all their territory. The British promised to provide the Indians with military support for the campaign against their Ameri-

War of 1812. Again the Wyandot disagreed about the selection of an ally. Most of those living near Sandusky chose to side with the United States; most living near Detroit, with England. Some Detroit Wyandot joined the Indian forces led by Tecumseh, the Shawnee chief, in battles against Americans.

Following Britain's defeat in this war, the U.S. government negotiated several more Wyandot land cessions. In the Treaty of the Rapids of Maumee of 1817, all the Indians in Ohio agreed to give up most of their remaining land there. The Wyandot were able to retain only two small reservations: Grand Reserve, which was located about 50 miles southwest of Sandusky in the area known as Upper Sandusky, and Big Spring Reservation, which was several miles to the northwest of Grand Reserve. In the Treaty of St. Mary's, signed in 1818, they also ceded the land they still held on the outskirts of Detroit in exchange for a small reservation of 5,000 acres on the Huron River in Michigan Territory.

But these reservations also soon became a target of settlers. Now there was pressure throughout the United States

*A 1833 lithograph by John Dorival of the death of Tecumseh, the leader of the western Indian confederacy, at the Battle of the Thames in 1813.*

for Indians to move west of the Mississippi River. The Indian Removal Act of 1830, passed by the U.S. Congress during the administration of President Andrew Jackson, required all eastern Indians to remove (relocate) to western lands assigned to them by the government. Land in what are now Oklahoma, Kansas, and Nebraska was set aside for this purpose and designated as Indian Territory. Although the Wyandot did not want to remove, they sent an advance delegation to examine the tract the government wanted to assign to them in present-day Kansas. When these delegates returned, they reported to their people that the area was unsuitable for farming and that the best land in Indian Territory was already occupied by other tribes.

The Wyandot continued to resist leaving the East, but they did agree gradually to sell their reservation land there. In 1832 the United States purchased Big Spring Reservation; in 1836, it bought the tract the Wyandot obtained through the Treaty of St. Mary's and most of Grand Reserve. Finally, under pressure from the federal government, the Wyandot sold their remaining land in Ohio in 1843, and their entire population of more than 700 removed to Indian Territory.

The previous year the U.S. government had agreed to allow the Wyandot to settle on any unoccupied tract of 148,000 acres of Indian Territory land they chose rather than on the land that their advance delegation had found inadequate to their needs. The Wyandot,

however, could not find an area of that size that was suitable and therefore decided instead to buy 25,260 acres of land near the Missouri and Kansas rivers from the Lenape Indians. The United States approved this purchase in 1848.

The Wyandot soon discovered that even their new property in Indian Ter-

*Mother Solomon, the last Wyandot resident of Upper Sandusky, photographed in 1887. Unlike most of her fellow tribespeople, she refused to move to Indian Territory in 1843.*

ritory was not safe from encroachment by non-Indian settlers. In 1854, Congress passed the Kansas-Nebraska Act, which created Kansas Territory and Nebraska Territory from the northern half of Indian Territory and opened up this area for American settlement. The government negotiated a treaty with the Wyandot the next year in which the Indians agreed to divide their commonly held land into individually owned plots, known as allotments. The male head of each household was to be given a 40-acre tract. This treaty also dissolved the Wyandot's government and made the Indians American citizens. As such, they lost their right to make claims for Indian land in the future.

To escape the influx of settlers into Kansas Territory, about 200 Wyandot within the next few years sold their allotments and traveled south to Indian Territory, which had been reduced to the area that is now Oklahoma. In 1858 the Seneca Indians agreed to sell these Wyandot a small 20,000-acre portion of their reservation in the northeastern corner of the region. Congress later recognized this agreement in the Omnibus Treaty of 1867 and offered the Wyandot remaining in Kansas the opportunity to sell their land and join their kin on the new reservation. The treaty also reestablished the Indian status of the Wyandot in Indian Territory. With this legal designation, these Wyandot lost their U.S. citizenship, but they became exempt from paying taxes on their land, which was again held in common as property of the clans.

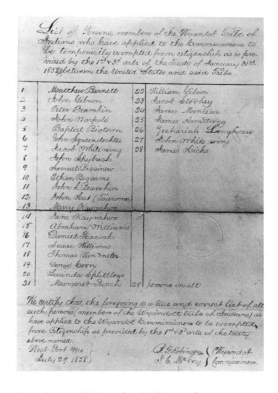

*A register of Wyandot Indians who were exempted from U.S. citizenship in the tribe's 1858 agreement with the Seneca. This list consisted of people who either chose to retain their legal status as Indians or were deemed by American officials to be "incompetent" to conduct their own affairs.*

At this time, the Canadian Wyandot came under the control of the government the British formed in 1867 to rule over the entire Dominion of Canada. Within the next decade, the Canadian government had developed a new policy toward the Indians living in its boundaries, which it set forth in the Indian Act of 1876. Under the act's provisions, tribes could become enfran-

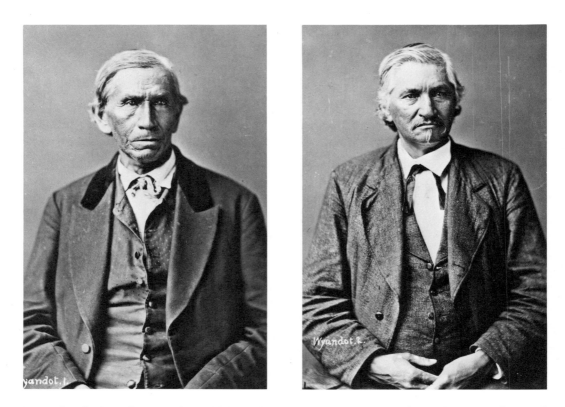

*Wyandot chief Mathew Mudeater (left) and tribal council member Nicholas Cotter. Both served as delegates to Washington, D.C., from Indian Territory in 1875.*

chised citizens of Canada, with the right to vote in the nation's elections. Enfranchised Indians were no longer permitted to have communal ownership of tax-free reserve lands. This territory would instead be divided into tracts, one of which became the privately owned property of the head of each household in the tribe.

The Canadian Wyandot were enfranchised in 1881. The land the Wyandot still retained at the Anderdon Reserve was then divided into 50-acre tracts, one of which was given to each of the 41 remaining families. With no commonly held land, the Canadian Wyandot soon lost their sense of unity. Gradually, they ceased to observe their ancient traditions as they adopted the customs of mainstream Canadian non-Indian society.

The western Wyandot retained their reservation in Indian Territory until 1890, when their land, too, was divided into individually owned allotments. Three years earlier the U.S. Congress had passed the General Allotment Act, which gave the president the right to allot all reservations in the western half of Indian Territory; in 1890 this portion of Indian Territory was named Oklahoma Territory. The government hoped that, as landowners, Indians would be able to become part of the mainstream of American society more easily. It also put the allotment policy into action in order to make Indian-owned land more available for use and settlement by non-Indians. Because the Wyandot lived in northeastern Indian Territory, the General Allotment Act did not apply to their land. Its enactment, however, made it clear to the tribe that the allotment of their territory was inevitable.

Believing that they had no other choice, the Wyandot in 1890 signed an allotment treaty by which the head of each Wyandot family received a tract of 160 acres. Once again they became private-property owners. The tribal government was disbanded, and the Wyandot people lost their legal status as Indians. In 1907 the reduced Indian Territory and Oklahoma Territory officially became the state of Oklahoma.

Long before these Wyandot lost their reservation, they had already begun to adopt the customs of their non-Indian neighbors. This occurred in part because their removal to Indian Territory had completely altered their econ-

*A school on the Seneca reservation in Indian Territory in 1890. Wyandot children attended classes in the building with the bell tower.*

*Students in the first through eighth grade attending the Seneca Indian School in 1887. The education Wyandot children received at this institution was intended to make them abandon their traditional values and adopt the ways of non-Indian Americans.*

omy. In the 19th century, the fur trade disappeared. In their western lands the Wyandot once again turned to farming for their livelihood. But in this unfamiliar terrain they abandoned their traditional agricultural techniques and instead began to use American tools, plows, and horses to help them farm their land. Following the example of non-Indian farmers, Wyandot men took over the traditionally female tasks of planting and harvesting. They also began to keep livestock, such as cattle, sheep, and pigs, to supplement their produce.

As the Wyandot's contact with non-Indians increased, they adopted other elements of American culture, such as clothing and housing styles. A minority of Wyandot also started to practice the religion of their neighbors after Protestant ministers began to establish missions among them in the early 19th century. Although the Indians initially resisted their teachings, gradually some Wyandot became Presbyterians or Methodists.

But it was the allotment of their Indian Territory reservation that caused the most rapid changes in Wyandot culture. Through all their migrations, clans had remained the center of their social and political life. But the significance of the clans, the traditional owners of Wyandot territory, was greatly decreased when the tribal lands were divided. Because the Wyandot were no longer permitted to have their own government, the clan leaders also lost their power over their people. These traditional social groupings soon broke apart. The disintegration of their clans further hastened the Wyandot's assimilation into the mainstream of American society.

Some distinctive elements of Wyandot culture have survived into the 20th century. Although most Wyandot have adopted Christianity, they still hold on to some Wendat religious beliefs. Many also continue to share with their children their ancestors' ancient stories of the early Wendat people. Despite their assimilation into non-Indian culture, the Wyandot in this way try to keep many of their traditional values alive. ▲

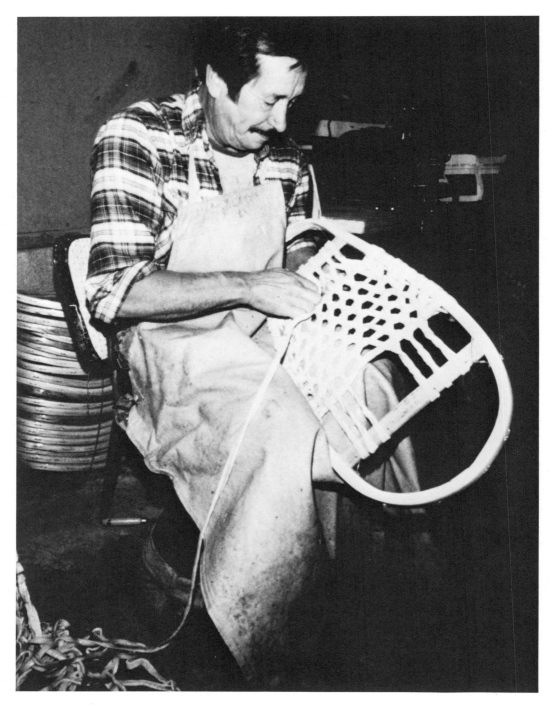

*Philippe Gros-Louis making a snowshoe in one of Wendake's workshops in 1983.*

# 7

# THE HURON
## AND
# THE WYANDOT TODAY

In most ways the lives of the Huron and Wyandot in the 20th century have been similar to those of their non-Indian neighbors. Outwardly, their languages, jobs, housing, and clothing have blended with the general pattern of Canadian and American culture. But in recent years both groups have come increasingly to appreciate their traditions. The Huron people in Canada and the United States today are proud of their heritage and of the role their ancestors played in the history of North America.

During the first half of this century, the Huron community at Wendake (Land of the Wendat), as the reserve near Quebec is now called, decreased significantly in size and population. More and more Huron left the reservation to live in towns and cities throughout the United States and Canada. The tribe sold much of its land to non-Indian Canadian neighbors. Other portions of their territory were confiscated by the Canadian government in the 1960s for the creation of parks and

the construction of the national Canadian railroad. By the last years of that decade, Wendake had dwindled to a mere 26 acres.

In 1968, Huron leaders concluded that they needed much more land if their community was to survive. Arguing that in the past the Huron had been illegally forced to cede much of the territory to which they had been entitled, they convinced the Canadian government to expand the boundaries of their territory. The government awarded the Huron a plot of land adjacent to their old reserve, which enlarged the size of Wendake to 143½ acres.

Visitors to Wendake today can immediately recognize which area is the original reserve and which is the recent addition. In the older section, narrow streets are lined with closely spaced houses and stores that sell handicrafts, such as baskets and embroidered clothing. Several workshops there manufacture a total of approximately 50,000 pairs of snowshoes and 3,000 canvas

*The workshop of canoe manufacturer Maurice Picard in 1983. Wendake residents produce more than 3,000 canoes annually for sale in the United States and Canada.*

canoes annually for sale throughout Canada and the United States. The old reserve is also the location of the Huron Museum, which displays the work of modern artisans alongside traditional tools, utensils, and garments. Another reminder of the area's history is Nôtre-Dame-de-Lorette, a Catholic church that was built in 1865 on a foundation constructed in 1730.

The newer section of Wendake reflects the economic prosperity of this growing community, which has one of the highest standards of living of all In-

dian reserves in Canada. Along its tree-lined streets and avenues are modern houses of all sizes and styles. The Huron Elementary School is also located in this area. Children who live in Wendake attend this institution for grades one through four. Beginning in the fifth grade, students go to schools a short distance away in Loretteville or Quebec.

Wendake residents have various means of employment. Some people work as artisans in the handicraft and manufacturing shops. Others own small businesses or stores that sell groceries, clothing, and other goods to residents and people traveling along Route 369, the highway that cuts through the reserve. Other Huron commute to nearby towns or Quebec for jobs in factories and businesses. Several Wendake residents have become prominent doctors, musicians, and artists.

Wendake is governed by the Huron National Council, whose headquarters are located in the old reserve area. The council is composed of five officials elected by the voters of Wendake for two-year terms. One member is elected as the chief councillor and presides over all council meetings. The major responsiblities of the council include overseeing the administration of the reserve and passing legislation regarding community matters. It presently manages a program funded by the Canadian government that provides low-interest loans for the construction of homes. The council also works with local doctors and nurses to improve the quality of health care available on the reserve.

In 1988 the resident population of Wendake was 959. In addition, 1,051 other Huron lived outside of the reserve in Canada or the United States. Recently the earlier trend of migration from the reserve has reversed as many people have returned to the Wendake from other localities. Because Wendake's population is relatively young (approximately one-third of all residents are less than 16 years old), the number of people living on the reserve will probably grow in the future.

In the late 1960s and 1970s, many Indian peoples throughout North America began to investigate their history and reassert their tribal identity. Along with 36 other bands (as Indian groups are now known in Canada), the Huron at Wendake participated in this movement by helping to form the Association of Indians of Quebec. This organization is dedicated to improving living conditions on all reserves in Quebec, protecting Indians' rights to hunt and fish in the region, and teaching the various groups involved about the others' traditions.

Two residents of Wendake have recently contributed to these educational efforts by writing books about Huron life today and in the past. In his 1973 autobiography, *First Among the Hurons*, Max Gros-Louis examines the changes on the reserve since his childhood. The book also urges the Huron to take political action to correct past injustices committed against them by the Canadian government, especially the forced cession of their land. Gros-Louis himself has worked toward this goal as an active member of the Association of Indians of Quebec and as a founder of the National Indian Brotherhood of Canada, which protects Indian land claims and fishing rights and awards college scholarships to Indian students. From 1964 to 1984, he served as the chief councillor of the Huron Nation and was reelected to this position in 1987.

Marguerite Vincent's *La Nation Huronne* (The Huron Nation), published in 1984, recounts the history of the Huron

# A PLEA FOR JUSTICE

*In recent years, the Huron of Wendake have fought increasingly with the Canadian government for the title to the lands of their original reserve and for the restoration of their hunting and fishing rights in the surrounding region. Perhaps their most ardent advocate is Max Gros-Louis, who has served as great chief of the Huron band for more than 20 years. In his 1974 autobiography,* First Among the Hurons, *Gros-Louis described the many injustices committed against him and the other inhabitants of Wendake by their non-Indian neighbors in recent years. He also voiced his people's frustrations with the Canadian government in the past and present as he called for the formation of new Indian policies in the future.*

"When the French first landed here in the sixteenth century, completely ignorant of our language, our customs, of our race itself, they were welcomed by my ancestors. . . . The result of the Hurons' loyal cooperation was the seizure of their lands. Now when Indians and Canadians come together we say to those who have become our enemies: 'When you arrived on this continent you had the missals and we had the land. And now, after abandoning your religion or changing it to suit your selfish needs, you have the land and we have the missals.'

"They tell us in reply that they gave us the right to vote in their democracy. But what does this right have to do with us? It was withheld until they were the majority. What is the meaning of the right to vote, belatedly bestowed on us, in elections for offices to which no Indian can aspire? English and French Canadians argue among themselves, trying to secure the best places, with no ideal except the money and the ecclesiastical revenues they might obtain. We are too proud to lower ourselves to discuss such frivolities. You can keep your right to vote, gentleman: just give us back our land! Don't accuse us of constantly disputing or of having revolutionary ideas. All I ask on behalf of all the Indians is the restitution of our natural rights which were taken from us by armed force at a time when strength constituted the only law that governed how people treated one another. But all that has changed and now when most of Africa has regained its political freedom who can criticize us for demanding that North America, the great spokesman for decolonization, should set a good example for the rest of the world?"

*Huron chief Max Gros-Louis speaking out for Indian rights during a 1988 press conference.*

people in Huronia and their subsequent migrations. Vincent records in her book traditional folktales and songs and includes a dictionary of Huron words in an effort to educate the people about their own culture.

This is also an intention of the Huron Elementary School Board. Its members are overseeing the development of a curriculum about the Huron's traditions and history for use in the school. Teachers there have already begun to instruct students in the basic vocabulary of the old Huron language.

Unlike their Canadian kin, the 3,045 official members of the Wyandot tribe of the United States do not live in or near a single community. They no longer have a reservation, but since the late 19th century they have retained tribal ownership of a 188-acre tract near the small town of Wyandotte, Oklahoma. Three hundred and fifty Wyandot live on this land and 500 reside elsewhere in the state. But the majority of the Wyandot today have scattered to towns and cities throughout the United States and Canada.

*Wyandot second chief Jim Bland (left) and chief Leaford Bearskin handing out leaflets to passerby Karen Sweeten in 1986. The Wyandot leaders were protesting restrictions that made health care at an Indian health center in Miami, Oklahoma, available only to people of one-quarter or more Indian ancestry.*

The community at Wyandotte looks to the Wyandot Council for leadership. This organization consists of six members—a chief, a second chief, and four councillors—and operates from the Wyandot Tribal Center in the town. The six representatives are elected by tribe members for two-year terms. At least once a month, the council holds open meetings in which everyone in the Wyandotte community can participate in discussions about local concerns. Annually, it conducts a special general meeting to elect new council members. The election is then followed by a community celebration.

The primary duty of the council is to monitor federal programs aimed at improving the Wyandot's standard of living. Through one of these programs, the council provides loans to tribal members for the construction or renovation of homes. Through another, it offers financial aid to the impoverished or the unemployed. The council also oversees the spending of funds granted by the federal government specifically for the education of Indian children. In the future, the Wyandot Council hopes to develop new programs, including ones that would enhance the tribal income and increase the economic self-sufficiency of individuals in the community.

The Oklahoma Wyandot are also striving to improve their health care. They are particularly concerned with the prevention and treatment of diabetes and heart ailments, which are prevalent among many American Indian groups. A clinic staffed by two doctors was recently built in Wyandotte, but to receive care for serious illnesses and injuries the Wyandot living there must travel more than 500 miles to the Indian Health Service Hospital in Claremont, Oklahoma.

Although today the Wyandot and the Huron have little contact with one another, they are still united by their common history as descendants of what was once one of the most powerful Indian confederacies in North America. Both groups share, too, an ability to survive. From the 17th century to the present, French, British, and Americans have unleashed waves of change that shook the foundations of their society, forced them to flee their ancestral lands, and divided them culturally, geographically, and politically. Like other American Indians, their lives were disrupted for centuries by external forces over which they had little control, forces that rendered it nearly impossible to maintain their traditional way of life. Nevertheless, the Huron and the Wyandot, in different ways and in different places, still struggle to reestablish elements of Wendat culture.

To thrive in the modern world, the Huron and Wyandot now look both forward and backward. In the future, they hope to improve the conditions of their lives by actively participating in the political and economic processes that help to shape them. And from the past, they are rediscovering aspects of their unique traditional culture that enable them to live proudly in the present. ▲

# BIBLIOGRAPHY

Barbeau, Marius. "Huron-Wyandot Traditional Narratives." *National Museum of Canada Bulletin* 165 (1960).

Bonvillain, Nancy. "Missionary Role in French Colonial Expansion." *Man in the Northeast* 29 (1985): 1–14.

———. "The Iroquois and the Jesuits: Strategies of Influence and Resistance." *American Indian Culture and Research Journal* 10 (1) (1986): 29–42.

Champlain, Samuel de. *Voyages of Samuel de Champlain 1604–1618*. Edited by W. L. Grant. New York: Scribners, 1907.

Gros-Louis, Max. *First Among the Hurons*. Montreal: Harvest House, 1973.

Hawthorn, H. B. *A Survey of Contemporary Indians of Canada*. 2 vols. Ottawa: Department of Indian and Northern Affairs, 1967.

Kill, Robert W. *Cornplanters of the Eastern Woodlands*. Canadian Native Peoples Series. Ottawa: Nelson Publishers, 1986.

Sagard, Gabriel Theodat de. *Long Journey to the Country of the Huron*. Edited by George Wrong. Toronto: The Champlain Society, 1939.

Trigger, Bruce. *Huron: Farmers of the North*. New York: Holt, Rinehart & Winston, 1969.

Tuck, James. "Northern Iroquoian Prehistory." In *Handbook of North American Indians*. Vol. 15, *The Northeast*. Edited by Bruce Trigger. Washington, DC: Smithsonian Institution, 1978.

# THE HURON AT A GLANCE

TRIBES *Huron and Wyandot*

CULTURE AREA *Great Lakes*

GEOGRAPHY *Great Lakes region of southern Ontario, Canada*

LINGUISTIC FAMILY *Iroquoian*

CURRENT POPULATION *Huron: approximately 1,890;
Wyandot: approximately 3,000*

FIRST CONTACT *Probably Samuel de Champlain, French, 1609*

FEDERAL STATUS *Huron: recognized, Canadian Band (tribal)
status. Most Huron live on a reserve (Wendake)
approximately six miles northwest of Quebec, Canada.
Wyandot: recognized, U.S. federal status. The Wyandot are
scattered across the United States, although many live on or
near their former reservation in northeastern Oklahoma.*

# GLOSSARY

**agent** A person appointed by the Bureau of Indian Affairs to supervise U.S. government programs on a reservation and/or in a specific region. After 1908 the title "superintendent" replaced "agent."

**Algonkian** The Indian peoples living in the northeastern United States and east-central Canada who speak Algonquian languages and share other cultural characteristics.

**Algonquian** The languages spoken by many Indian peoples in northeastern North America, including the Algonquin, the Nipissing, and other tribes that lived geographically close to the Huron.

**Algonquin** A tribal group living in the Ottawa River valley region of Canada. Traditional trading partners of the Huron.

**allotment** U.S. policy, first applied on a large scale after passage of the General Allotment Act in 1887, to break up tribally owned reservations by assigning individual farms and ranches to Indians. Intended as much to discourage traditional communal activities as to encourage private farming and assimilate Indians into mainstream American life.

**archaeology** The recovery and study of evidence of past human ways of life, especially that of prehistoric peoples but also that of historic peoples.

**band** A loosely organized group of people who live in one area and are bound together by the need for food and defense, by family ties, or by other common interests. Also, the term used in Canada today to denote Indian tribes.

**blood feud** A form of justice in which relatives avenged the death of a family member by killing the murderer or a member of his family. Huron blood feuds sometimes continued for many years.

**Bureau of Indian Affairs (BIA)** A U.S. government agency within the Department of the Interior. Originally intended to manage trade and other relations with Indians, the BIA now seeks to develop and implement programs that encourage Indians to manage their own affairs and to improve their educational opportunities and general social and economic well-being.

**clan** A multigenerational group having a shared identity, organization, and property, based on belief in their descent from a common ancestor.

Because clan members consider themselves closely related, marriage within a clan is strictly prohibited.

**confederacy** Union of related tribes or nations that functions as a political, military and/or economic unit.

**culture** The learned behavior of humans; nonbiological, socially taught activities; the way of life of a group of people.

**curers** Members of the Huron tribe who diagnosed and treated diseases through rituals and natural medicines and were believed to have supernatural powers.

**Feast of the Dead** Iroquoian ceremony, held by the Huron about every 10 years, during which the bones of all people who had died since the previous ceremony were unearthed and reburied in a common grave (ossuary).

**fur trade** Trading network in North America through which Indians gave Europeans animal pelts in exchange for manufactured goods. The Huron prospered economically by trading beaver pelts to the French during the 16th and 17th centuries.

**Huron** Name for the Wendat used after the early 17th century. French explorers and traders first called them Huron, which means "rough" or "unkempt."

**Huronia** Region in southwestern Ontario between Georgian Bay and Lake Simcoe that was the original homeland of the Huron tribe.

**Indian Territory** An area in the south-central United States where the U.S. government wanted to resettle Indians from other regions, especially the eastern states. In 1907, the territory became the state of Oklahoma.

**Iroquoian** The family of languages spoken by a group of related Indian tribes in the Northeast, including the Huron, Petun, Neutrals, Erie, and the six Iroquois Nations; also, the groups speaking these languages.

**Jesuit** A member of the Society of Jesus, a Roman Catholic order founded by Saint Ignatius Loyola in 1534. The Jesuits are highly learned and, in the 17th century, were particularly active in spreading Christianity outside Europe.

**longhouse** House structure with a frame made of

cedar covered with bark and branches, in which most members of Iroquoian tribes, including the Huron, lived. These dwellings were sometimes 100 feet long and could house 10 or 12 families.

*matrilineal descent* Rules for determining family or clan membership by tracing kinship through female ancestors.

*matrons* Respected elder women of Huron clans. Matrons were responsible for supervising their clan members' household and agricultural work and for choosing clan chiefs.

*oki* Supernatural power, which the Huron believed some elements (such as the sky and sun) and people possessed.

*Ononharoia* Huron word literally meaning "turning the brain upside down." Used to describe an annual Huron ceremony during which the members of the tribe tried to guess and grant each other's secret desires by interpreting dreams.

*ossuary* Place in which the bones of many people are buried.

*palisade* Structure made of upright wooden poles surrounding a village or other settlement to protect it from enemy attack.

*prehistory* Anything that happened before written records existed for a given locality. In North America, anything earlier than the first contact with Europeans is considered to be prehistoric.

*proto-Iroquoian* Ancestral language spoken by all Iroquoian peoples.

*removal policy* Federal policy, begun in 1830, calling for the sale of all Indian land in the eastern and southern United States and for the relocation of Indians from these areas to lands west of the Mississippi River.

*reservation, reserve* A tract of land set aside by treaty for Indian occupation and use. "Reservation" is used to describe such lands in the United States; "reserve," in Canada.

*sagamite* Huron soup made from corn.

*subsistence* Methods of obtaining food for survival including food collection (gathering wild foods from the environment) and food production (cultivating plant foods and raising domestic livestock).

*territory* The governmental status of a defined region of the United States that is not, but may become, a state. The states of Kansas, Nebraska, and Oklahoma, among others, were once territories or parts of a territory.

*tribe* A society consisting of several or many separate communities united by kinship, culture, and language, and such other social factors as clans, religious organization, and economic and political institutions.

*trust* The relationship between the federal government and many Indian tribes, dating from the late 19th century. Government agents managed Indians' business dealings, including land transactions and rights to national resources, because the Indians were alleged to be legally incompetent to manage their own affairs.

*wampum* Shell beads used by tribes in the northeastern United States in strings or "belts" as a pledge of the truth of their words, symbols of high office, records of diplomatic negotiations and treaties, and records of other important events. From the Algonquian word *wampumpeag*, meaning "white (bead) strings."

*Wendat* Name that the Huron called themselves, literally meaning "Islanders" or "Dwellers on a Peninsula."

*Wyandot* Name of the branch of the Huron tribe that lived in the southern Great Lakes region in the mid-1700s and moved to Indian Territory in the 1840s. Today most of the Wyandot live in northeastern Oklahoma.

# INDEX

Aataentsic legend, 13
Act of Concession of 1651, 73
*Agnonha*, 42
Agriculture, 15–18, 21–22, 74
Albany, New York, 56, 83
Algonkian (tribes), 41–42, 48, 79
Algonquian language family, 41
Algonquin (tribe), 27
Allotment treaty, 93
American Revolution, 87
Ancienne Lorette, 64
Anderdon Reserve, 87–88, 92
Archaeology, 14
Arendahronon, 19, 42, 63
Association of Indians of Quebec, 101
Attignawantan, 19, 63
Attigneenongnahac, 19, 63
Awataerohi ceremony, 35–37

Beauport, 63–64
Beavers, 25, 41
Big Spring Reservation, 89, 90
Black River, 81
Blood feuds, 32
Braddock, Edward, 86
Brebéuf, Jean de, 51
British, trade with, 83, 85
Brulé, Étienne, 44

Cabane d'Automne, 75–76, 77
Cadillac, Antoine de, 83
Cartier, Jacques, 41
Cayuga, 42
Ceremonies: Awataerohi, 35–37; burial, 18; curing, 33–37; dance in, 33; death, 32, 36–39; marriage (*See* Marriage); tobacco in, 22, 25–26; warfare, 32; women in, 29
Champlain, Samuel de, 42, 43–44, 48
Charlevoix, Pierre de, 85
Chequamegon, 81

Chiefs, 29–30
Children: missionaries' attitudes toward, 52–53; socialization of, 29
Christianity, 52–54, 56, 59, 61, 76, 95
Clan system, 27; decline of, 76
Clothing, 24
Company of New France, 73
Corn, 21, 22, 24
Côte-St-Michel, 64
Councils, 29–32
Crawford, William, 87
Criminality, 53

Dance, 33
Death ceremonies, 32, 36–39
Detroit, 83, 85, 87, 89
Disease: *See* Measles; Small-pox
Dreams, 34–35; missionaries' ridiculing of, 53–54; significance in warfare, 44–45
Dutch, trade with, 49

Early Iroquoian period, 16–17
Eastern Woodland culture, 14
Epidemics, 54–55, 61
Erie, 19
Erie, Lake, 19, 83, 87

Fallen Timbers, 88
Farming, 15–17, 21–22, 74
Feast of the Dead, 38–39
Feasts, 32–33
*First Among the Hurons* (Gros-Louis), 101
Fishing, 24–25
Food: agricultural production of, 15–18
Fort Duquesne, 86
Fort Orange, 56. *See* also Albany
Fort Pitt, 86
Framing, 17–18
France: trade with, 41–49. *See also* Missionaries

Freedom, 29, 30; missionaries' attempt to change attitudes about, 52
French and Indian War, 86
Funerals. *See* Death ceremonies
Fur trade, 48–49

Gahoendoe, 61
Gandougare, 59
General Allotment Act, 92–93
Georgian Bay, 13, 59
Government, 29–32
Grand Reserve, 89, 90
Great Britain: relationship with, 75–77, 85–87; trade with, 83
Green Bay, 80
Greenville, Treaty of, 88
Gros-Louis, Max, 101

Homes, 16–17, 18. *See also* Longhouses
Households: women's role in, 24
Hudson River, 49, 83
Hunting, 25
Huron: dwelling, 76; Farming, 74; French use of term, 42; marriage practices of, 27, 29; modern population, 99–101. *See also* Huron-Petun; Wendat; Wyandot
Huron Confederacy: decline of, 59, 83
Huron Elementary School, 98, 101
Huronia, 42, 44, 51, 54, 55, 59, 61, 79, 81
Huron Island, 80. *See also* Rock Island
Huron, Lake, 80, 83
Huron language, 13; decline of, 76, 77
Huron Museum, 98
Huron National Council, 99
Huron-Petun: government, 83; westward migration of, 79–95

Illinois (tribe), 83
Illness: curing ceremonies, 33–37; epidemics, 54–55, 61; modern health-care facilities, 103
Indian Act of 1876 (Canada), 91–92
Indian Removal Act of 1830, 90
Indian Territory, 90–93, 94
Industry and labor, 98–99
Iouskeha, 13
Iron utensils, 41–42
Iroquoian language family, 15, 79
Iroquois, 49, 56–59, 63, 79–80, 82, 85
Iroquois Confederacy, 42; peace treaty with, 63–64; resettlement among, 59

Jackson, Andrew, 90
Jesuit missionaries, 51–54, 55–56, 73. *See also* Missionaries
Jeune Lorette, 64, 73

Kansas-Nebraska Act, 91
Kansas River, 90
Kansas Territory, 91

Lalemant, Gabriel, 55
Land cessions, 87–88
Land ownership, 27
Language. *See* Algonquian language family; Iroquoian language family; Wendat, language
Late Iroquoian period, 18–19
LeCaron, Joseph, 44, 51
LeMercier, Joseph, 56
Lenape, 83, 88, 90
Longhouses, 17, 18, 27
Louis XIII (king of France), 44

Marriage: matrilocal residence system, 27; missionaries' attempt to change customs, 52; protocol and ceremony, 27–29; selection of partners, 27

Measles, 54–55, 63
Michigan, Lake, 80
Michigan: migration to, 80
Michigan Territory, 89
Michilimackinac, 80, 81, 82–83
Middle Iroquoian period, 17–18
Missionaries, 21, 44, 48, 51–54; antagonism toward, 55–56; resettlement role of, 63–64, 73
Mohawk, 42–43, 56–57; peace treaty with, 63
Mohawk River, 49
Montreal, Quebec, 61

National Indian Brotherhood of Canada, 101
*Nation Huronne, La* (Vincent), 101
Neutrals, 19, 26–27, 59
New France, 51, 75
Nipissing, 27, 41, 48
Northwest Territory, 88
Nôtre-Dame-de-Foy, 64. *See also* Sainte-Foy

Oneida, 42
*Oki,* 32
Oklahoma Territory, 93
Onondaga, 59, 63
Ononharoia, 35, 53
Ontario, 13, 15–17, 79
Ontario, Lake, 19
Orleans: resettlement on, 63
Orontony, 85
Ossuaries, 18
Ottawa, 80, 83

Paris, Treaty of, 87
Petun, 19, 26–27, 59. *See also* Huron-Petun
Pontiac, 86–87
Potawatomi, 83
Pottery, 24
Pre-Iroquoian period, 15

Quarante Arpents, 75, 77
Quebec, 44, 51, 56–57, 64, 73, 74, 77; resettlement to, 61–63

Rapids of Maumee, the, Treaty of, 89
Recallet missionaries, 44, 48. *See also* Missionaries
Religion. *See* Missionaries
Reservations, 75, 89–90
Rituals. *See* Ceremonies
Rock Island, 80

*Sagamite,* 24
Sagard, Gabriel Theodat de, 44–48
Sainte-Foy, 64
Sainte-Marie, 56
St. Ignace, 82
St. Lawrence River, 41, 56–57, 61, 63
St. Mary's, Treaty of, 89
Sandusky, 85, 87–88, 89
Sandusky Bay, 85, 88
Sandusky River, 83
Savignon, 44
Seneca, 42, 58, 59, 91
Shawnee, 83, 88
Simcoe, Lake, 13
Sioux, 81–82
Smallpox, 54–55, 61, 63
Sunflower, 18
Superior, Lake, 80, 81

Tahontaenrat, 19, 59
Tawiscaron, 13
Tecumseh, 89
Tobacco: ceremonial use of, 22, 25–26; in warfare ceremonies, 32
Trade, 26–27, 31–32; with Britain, 83, 85; with Dutch, 49; with French, 41–49, 81, 83; of furs, 48–49; of manufactured goods, 74
Tribal divisions: formation of, 19

United States: first treaty with, 88; Wyandot's relationship with, 87–91

Villages, 16–17; councils, 29–32
Vincent, Marguerite, 101

Visitors: treatment of, 44–48

Warfare, 18; chiefs, 30; dreams' significance in, 44–45; French alliance, 42; with Iroquois Confederacy, 42, 56–57; warriors, 32
War of 1812, 89
Washington, George, 88
Wayne, Anthony, 88
Wendake, 97–101
Wendat: agriculture, 15–17, 17–18; clan system, 27; cosmology, 32; government, 29–32; land ownership, 27; language, 21; meaning of name, 13; origins, 13–19; population in 17th century, 21; postepidemic population, 54–55; social relationships, 27; trade with France, 41–49; villages, 16–17. *See also* Huron; Huron-Petun; Wyandot
Wendat Confederacy, 19, 31–32
Wisconsin: migration to, 81
Women: ceremonial role of, 29; chores and responsibilities of, 23–24; equal status of, 29; role in agriculture, 22; role in death ceremonies, 38
Wyandot: cultural changes and assimilation, 94–95; modern population of, 101; relationship with United States, 87–91; removal to west, 90–91; warfare with Britain, 86–87
Wyandot Council, 102–3
Wyandotte, 101–2
Wye River, 56

# PICTURE CREDITS

Archives Nationales de France (Paris), Fonds des Colonies, serie C 11a, vol. 9, fol. 43–43v, page 78; The Bettmann Archive, pages 50, 60, 82, 86; Canapress, page 101; Gagnon Collection, Bibliotheque Municipal de Montreal, Canada, page 64; Huntington Library, San Marino, California, MS #HM 29 (9), page 40; Kansas Collection, University of Kansas Libraries, page 91; Library of Congress, pages 24, 26, 31, 34, 38, 43, 46, 54, 80, 85; McCord Museum of Canadian History, Montreal, Canada, pages 33, 58; Miami, OK, *News-Record,* page 102; Museum of the American Indian/Heye Foundation, pages 49, 70 (bottom), 75, 76, 88; National Anthropological Archives, Smithsonian Institution, page 92 (neg. #973A, 975); National Geographic Society, James L. Stanfield, page 73; National Museum of Canada, cover, pages 17, 18, 23, 26, 33, 66, 68, 69, 70 (top and middle); New-York Historical Society, page 74; Peabody Museum, Harvard University, pages 67, 72; Public Archives of Canada, page 20; Royal Ontario Museum, pages 12, 14; SAA, pages 96 (photo by Jacques Nadeau), 98 (photo by Claire Dufour); Sainte-Marie Among the Hurons, Midland, Ontario, Canada, pages 16, 57; Western History Collections, University of Oklahoma Library, pages 90, 93, 94.

Maps (pages 2, 62, 84) by Gary Tong.

# ACKNOWLEDGMENTS

I wish to thank Mr. Leaford Bearskin, chief of the Wyandots in Oklahoma, and Dr. Charles Garrad of the Ontario Archaeological Society, for their generous help in providing information about the history and current circumstances of the Wyandot people. Thanks also to Mr. Roger Vincent, principal of the Huron Elementary School in Wendake, for his assistance.

NANCY BONVILLAIN is associate professor of anthropology at the State University of New York at Stony Brook. She has a Ph.D. in anthropology from Columbia University. Dr. Bonvillain has written a grammar and dictionary of the Mohawk language and has edited *Studies in Iroquois Culture* (1980). She has received grants from the National Endowment for the Humanities, the National Museum of Canada, and the American Philosophical Society for her research in 17th- and 18th-century Iroquoian history.

---

FRANK W. PORTER III, general editor of INDIANS OF NORTH AMERICA, is director of the Chelsea House Foundation for American Indian Studies. He holds a B.A., M.A., and Ph.D. from the University of Maryland. He has done extensive research concerning the Indians of Maryland and Delaware and is the author of numerous articles on their history, archaeology, geography, and ethnography. He was formerly director of the Maryland Commission on Indian Affairs and American Indian Research and Resource Institute, Gettysburg, Pennsylvania, and he has received grants from the Delaware Humanities Forum, the Maryland Committee for the Humanities, the Ford Foundation, and the National Endowment for the Humanities, among others. Dr. Porter is the author of *The Bureau of Indian Affairs* in the Chelsea House KNOW YOUR GOVERNMENT series.